Endless Sparkle

12 crystal components   unlimited jewelry designs

Aimee Carpenter

KB
KALMBACH BOOKS

Kalmbach Books
21027 Crossroads Circle
Waukesha, Wisconsin 53186
www.Kalmbach.com/Books

Illustrations by the author. All photography © 2011
Kalmbach Books.

Published in 2011
15 14 13 12 11   1 2 3 4 5

Manufactured in the United States of America

ISBN: 978-0-87116-422-3

Publisher's Cataloging-in-Publication Data

Carpenter, Aimee.
 Endless sparkle : 12 crystal components, unlimited jewelry
designs / Aimee Carpenter.

   p. : ill. (some col.) ; cm.

   ISBN: 978-0-87116-422-3

   1. Beadwork–Patterns. 2. Beadwork–Handbooks,
manuals, etc. 3. Jewelry making–Handbooks, manuals,
etc. I. Title.

TT860 .C27 2011
745.5942

Contents

Crystal Components

Finished Jewelry

Introduction

I have always loved beads! I did not have any actual skill with them, however, until I took my first class. It was at a local bead shop, the White Fox Bead Studio in Maryville, Tenn. The class was for a peyote-stitch bracelet. I remember thinking to myself, "Well, she can try to teach me, but there is no way I will ever be able to do this." I was so wrong, and from then on, I was hooked on beads. Over the next few years, I was able to take more classes and learn lots of new skills. One of the instructors taught a lot of classes using my favorite Swarovski crystals, which got me thinking...

I really love sparkly things. I wanted to make rings using crystals, so that I could look at the crystals all of the time. Unfortunately, ring designs were scarce. So, I started playing around with different ideas and came up with my own designs. At the time, it never crossed my mind to teach classes or to write up official instructions for these designs. People started asking me about my rings and where they could get the patterns. There were no patterns yet because they were all in my head. After some convincing, I agreed to start writing instructions and teaching classes.

Over time, I came up with more and more designs, so I started expanding the instructions to include things like matching earrings, pendants, etc. My friends started joking that I should have a book, so that led me here today.

HOW TO USE THIS BOOK

The pieces in this book are fun and easy to create. Begin with the first section, and pick your favorite crystal component. There are lots of styles to choose from— including whimsical, elegant, and romantic. After you create the component, flip to the second section to create a beautiful finished jewelry piece. I've offered suggestions for which components work best with the projects, but be creative! These sparkly bits go together in so many different ways.

With all the crystal shades available, the possibilities for color palettes are truly endless. Use my examples for inspiration, or create a masterpiece in your favorite hues. You don't need a lot of jewelry-making experience to complete them. Some beading knowledge is helpful, but I will guide you step by step. The most important thing is to have fun. If I can do it, you can too!

Materials & Tools

You only need a small pile of beads, a needle, and some thread to begin beading.

I primarily use **round and bicone-shaped crystals**. You can try crystals from many different manufacturers, including Swarovski, Czech Preciosa, and Crystazzi. I used Swarovski crystals for the projects in this book, as they are available in many different colors and shapes. You will use a lot of bicone crystals in 3 mm, 4 mm, 6 mm, and 8 mm sizes. Round crystals are fun for embellishing.

Seed beads come in different sizes, shapes, and colors. I use small size 11º seed beads and size 15º seed beads for these delicate jewelry pieces. Try using small **cylinder beads** for making peyote bails or getting a consistent shape in embellished loops.

I love **crystal pearls** because they are uniform and easy to stitch. Look for traditional round pearls and pearl drops. Again, these come in many different colors and sizes, so pick the pearls that fit your project.

For a glamorous option, try **crystal drops** instead of pearls. Cubic zirconia briolette drops are also a beautiful choice.

Wire ranges from 16- to 26-gauge, and it comes in many finishes. I love the look of sterling silver and gold-plated wire with crystals, but you can also try copper or colored craft wire for a fun and economical twist.

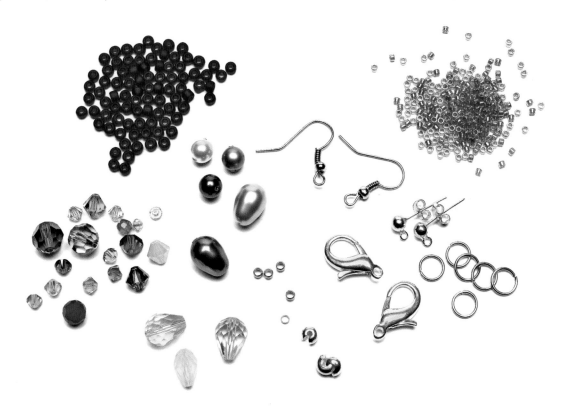

For stitching, I prefer **FireLine** GSP thread, originally developed as fishing line, because it is durable and won't be cut by the sharp edges of crystals. Plus, when you are reinforcing sections of crystal, you do not have to worry about your needle splitting the thread. FireLine comes in different thicknesses and colors (crystal and smoke). I prefer 4-lb. test. Use crystal for light-colored beads, and use smoke for dark beads.

Use **beading wire or stringing wire** to string your beads and attach clasps. Beading wire comes in various sizes and colors. I use 49-strand, .019 size wire. It is strong and still very flexible.

FInish your jewelry with **crimps**, thin tubes that are flattened to hold beading wire in place. A **crimp cover** is a C-Shaped bead that you put over a crimp bead in order to disguise it to look like a regular round bead.

Choose **ear wires**, **clasps**, **jump rings**, and other **findings** in various finishes to complement your crystals and give your jewelry a professional polish.

Size 12 beading needles are small enough to use with tiny seed beads but are still easy to thread.

Use a small, sharp pair of **scissors** to cut FireLine and other beading thread.

A **thread burner** is one of my favorite tools. Use it to trim thread close to your beads. Scissors and nippers won't trim thread so close and clean.

Use **crimping pliers** to crimp the crimp beads around beading wire.

Chainnose pliers are used for many beading needs, such as manipulating the wire for a wrapped-loop bail. Use chainnose pliers to apply a crimp cover over a crimp bead or to open and close loops.

Use **roundnose pliers** to create plain and wrapped loops from wire.

Use **wire cutters** to trim excess wire. They are also helpful for trimming beading wire after you have applied a crimp bead.

Beading mats are rectangular-shaped pieces of fabric used as a work space for your beading. They are great because you can stab your needles in them so you don't lose them. The surface also keeps your tiny beads from rolling all over the place.

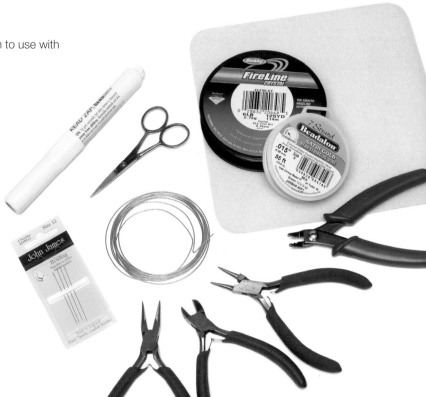

Jewelry-making Basics

Before you begin, it's helpful to review some basic jewelry-making techniques. Practice making a few loops or knots if you like, or just dive right in to the projects. Refer back to this section as needed.

Conditioning thread

If you use a thread other than FireLine, use either beeswax (not candle wax or paraffin) or Thread Heaven to condition that thread. Beeswax smooths the nylon fibers and adds tackiness that will stiffen your bead-work slightly. Thread Heaven adds a static charge that causes the thread to repel itself, so don't use it with doubled thread. Stretch the thread, then pull it through the conditioner, starting with the end that comes off the spool first.

Ending/adding thread

To end a thread, weave back into the beadwork, following the existing thread path and tying two or three half-hitch knots around the thread between beads as you go. Change directions as you weave so the thread crosses itself. Sew through a few beads after the last knot before cutting the thread. To add a thread, start several rows below the point where the last bead was added, and weave through the beadwork, tying half-hitch knots between beads.

Reinforcing

Pass your needle back through beads you just added to strengthen your design and tighten up tension. I usually do this two or three times. If you are using very small seed beads, reinforce only once.

Half-hitch knot

Pass the needle under the thread between two beads. A loop will form as you pull the thread through. Cross over the thread between the beads, sew through the loop, and pull gently to draw the knot into the beadwork.

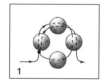

Overhand knot

Make a loop at the end of the thread. Pull the short tail through the loop, and tighten.

Square knot

Bring the left-hand thread over the right-hand thread and around. Cross right over left, and go through the loop. Pull to tighten.

Right-angle weave

1 To start the first row, pick up four beads, and tie into a ring. Go through the first three beads again.
2 Pick up three beads. Go back through the last bead of the previous ring (**a–b**) and continue through the first two picked up for this stitch (**b–c**).
3 Continue adding three beads for each stitch until the first row is the desired length. You are sewing rings in a figure 8 pattern, alternating direction with each stitch.

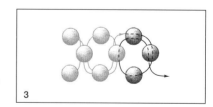

4. To begin row 2, go through the last three beads of the last stitch on row 1, exiting the bead at the edge of one long side.

5. Pick up three beads, and go back through the bead you exited in the previous step **(a–b)**. Continue through the first new bead **(b–c)**.

6. Pick up two beads, and go through the next top bead on the previous row and the bead you exited on the previous stitch **(a–b)**. Continue through the two new beads and the next top bead of the previous row **(b–c)**.

7. Pick up two beads, go through bead you exited on the previous stitch, the top bead on the previous row, and the first new bead. Keep the thread moving in a figure 8. Pick up two beads per stitch for the rest of the row. When you go back through, don't sew straight lines across stitches.

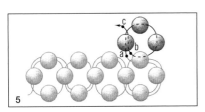

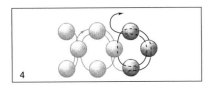

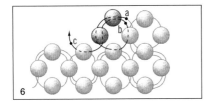

Peyote stitch, flat even-count

1. Pick up an even number of beads **(a–b)**. These beads will shift to form the first two rows.

2. To begin row 3, pick up a bead, skip the last bead strung in the previous step, and sew through the next bead in the opposite direction **(b–c)**. For each stitch, pick up a bead, skip a bead in the previous row, and sew through the next bead, exiting the first bead strung **(c–d)**. The beads added in this row are higher than the previous rows and are referred to as "up-beads."

3. For each stitch in subsequent rows, pick up a bead, and sew through the next up-bead in the previous row **(d–e)**. To count peyote stitch rows, count the total number of beads along both straight edges.

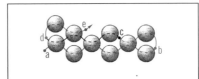

Flattened crimp

1. Hold the crimp using the tip of your chainnose pliers. Squeeze the pliers firmly to flatten the crimp.

2. Tug the wire to make sure the crimp has a solid grip. If the wire slides, repeat the steps with a new crimp.

Folded crimp

1. Position the crimp bead in the notch of the crimping pliers that is closest to the handle. Holding the wires apart, squeeze the tool to compress the crimp bead, making sure one wire is on each side of the dent.

2. Place the crimp bead in the front notch of the tool, and position it so the dent is facing outward. Squeeze the tool to fold the crimp in half.

3. Tug on the wires to ensure that the crimp is secure.

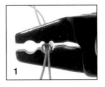

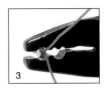

Crimp cover

Place the crimp cover over the folded crimp bead, and use chainnose pliers to gently squeeze the cover in place.

Plain loops

1. Trim the wire ¼ in. (6 mm) above the last bead strung. Using chainnose pliers, make a right-angle bend above the bead.

2. Grip the tip of the wire in roundnose pliers. Press downward slightly, and rotate the wire into a loop.

3. Let go, then grip the loop at the same place on the pliers, and keep turning to close the loop. The closer to the tip that you work, the smaller the loop will be.

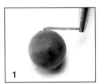

Opening and closing loops

1. Hold the loop or jump ring with two pairs of chainnose pliers or chainnose and roundnose pliers, as shown.

2. To open the loop or jump ring, bring one pair of pliers toward you and push the other pair away. String materials on the open loop or jump ring. Reverse the steps to close the open loop or jump ring.

Wrapped loops

1. Make sure you have at least 1¼ in. (3.2 cm) of wire above the last bead strung. With the tip of your chainnose pliers, grasp the wire above the bead. Bend the wire (above the pliers) into a right angle.

2. Using roundnose pliers, position the jaws in the bend.

3. Bring the wire over the top jaw of the roundnose pliers.

4. Reposition the pliers' lower jaw snugly into the loop. Curve the wire downward around the bottom of the roundnose pliers. This is the first half of a wrapped loop.

5. Position the chainnose pliers' jaws across the loop.

6. Wrap the wire around the wire stem, covering the wire between the loop and the top bead. Trim the excess wire and press the cut end close to the wraps with chainnose pliers.

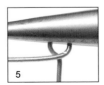

Wrapping above a top-drilled bead or crystal

1. Center a top-drilled bead or crystal on a 3-in. (7.6 cm) piece of wire. Bend each wire end upward, crossing them into an X above the bead.

2. Using chainnose pliers, make a small bend in each wire end so they form a right angle.

3. Wrap the horizontal wire around the vertical wire as in a wrapped loop. Trim the excess wrapping wire.

4. Make a loop with the vertical wire directly above these wraps.

Crystal

Components

To create fun and easy stitched jewelry, begin with a basic crystal component and build it into a larger jewelry piece. Each component taught is pictured in a finished jewelry design; once you've stitched the foundation, turn to the second section to complete your piece. Have fun!

Keepsake

Projects
To finish the jewelry shown for this component, turn to Double-trouble Earrings, p. 70, or Centerpiece Ring, p. 92.

This design reminds me of a keepsake box, with the center crystal acting as the lock. A simple and quick design, it offers plenty of options for experimenting with color.

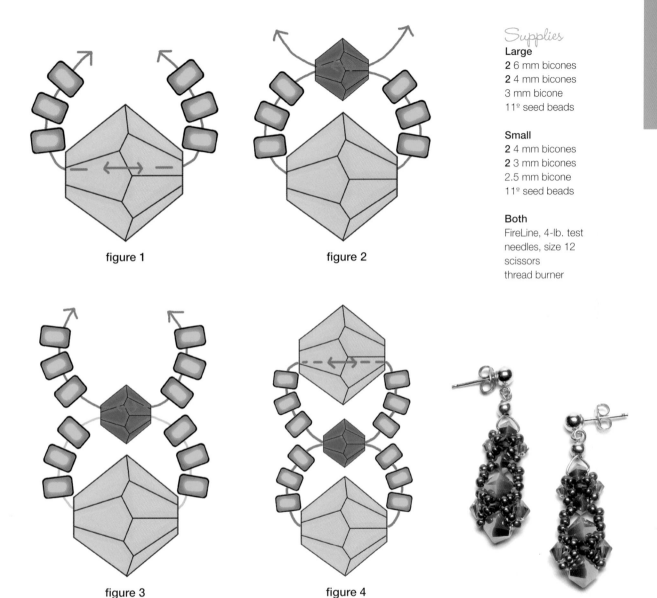

figure 1

figure 2

figure 3

figure 4

Supplies

Large
2 6 mm bicones
2 4 mm bicones
3 mm bicone
11º seed beads

Small
2 4 mm bicones
2 3 mm bicones
2.5 mm bicone
11º seed beads

Both
FireLine, 4-lb. test
needles, size 12
scissors
thread burner

NOTE: For the small component, substitute 4 mm bicones for 6 mm bicones, 3 mm bicones for 4 mm bicones, and a 2.5 mm bicone for a 3 mm bicone.

1. Cut about 1 yd. (.9 m) of thread and thread a needle on both ends.

2. Pick up a 6 mm bicone and center it on the thread. Pick up three 11º seed beads on each side **[figure 1]**.

3. Pick up a 3 mm bicone with one needle, then pass the other needle through the 3 mm bicone in the opposite direction **[figure 2]**.

4. Pick up three 11º seed beads on each side **[figure 3]**.

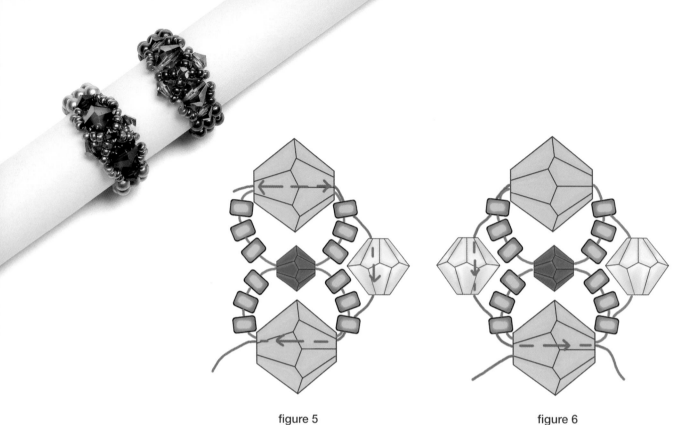

figure 5

figure 6

5. Pick up another 6 mm bicone with one needle, then pass the other needle through the 6 mm bicone, going in the opposite direction **[figure 4]**.

6. The thread will now be exiting both sides of the top 6 mm bicone. Pass one of the needles through the top 11º. Pick up a 4 mm bicone and pass the needle through the bottom 11º and the bottom 6 mm bicone **[figure 5]**.

7. Repeat step 6 with the other needle **[figure 6]**. The needles will be exiting the bottom 6 mm bicone in opposite directions.

8. Reinforce the component by passing the needles back through the first three 11º seed beads, the 3 mm bicone, the next three 11ºs, the top 6 mm bicone, the top 11ºs, the 4 mm bicones, and the bottom 6 mm bicone on each side **[figure 7]**.

figure 7

Vintage Elegance

Projects
To finish the jewelry shown for this component, turn to Pearl Drop Earrings, p. 60, Linked Bracelet, p. 63, Chandelier Necklace, p. 79, or Centerpiece Ring, p. 92.

Evoke the shapes of nature with floral, vine-like jewelry. This beautiful, delicate design was inspired by vintage jewelry, and it is perfect for any occasion or wardrobe.

6 mm bicone or round crystal
8 4 mm bicones
12 3 mm bicones
11º seed beads
FireLine, 4-lb. test
needles, size 12
scissors
thread burner

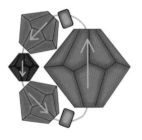

figure 1

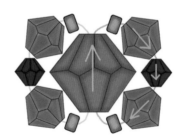

figure 2

figure 3

1. Cut about 1 yd. (.9 m) of thread, and thread a needle.

2. Pick up a 6 mm bicone or round crystal and slide it down the thread, leaving an 8-in. (20 cm) tail.

3. Pick up one 11º seed bead, one 4 mm bicone, one 3 mm bicone, one 4 mm bicone, and one 11º. Pass the needle back up through the 6 mm bicone **[figure 1]**. Pass the needle back through these beads to reinforce.

4. Repeat step 3 on the other side of the 6 mm bicone or round **[figure 2]**.

5. Passing the needle through the beads surrounding the 6 mm bicone, add a 3 mm bicone in between the bottom 11º seed beads and the top 11º seed beads **[figure 3]**. Reinforce, exiting a 4 mm bicone.

6. Pick up one 3 mm bicone, one 4 mm bicone, and one 3 mm bicone.

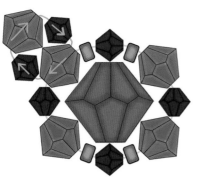

figure 4

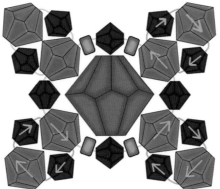

figure 5

7. Pass the needle through the other side of the first 4 mm bicone **[figure 4]**. Reinforce a few times.

8. Repeat step 6 three more times around the design **[figure 5]**. Reinforce as you go.

Heirloom

Create a beautiful, unique piece of jewelry to be handed down from generation to generation. This elegant piece transcends time and trends.

Projects

To finish the jewelry shown for this component, turn to Pearl Drop Earrings, p. 60, Drop Pendant, p. 66, or Centerpiece Ring, p. 92.

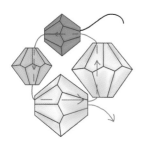

figure 1

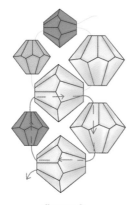

figure 2

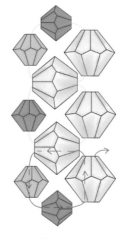

figure 3

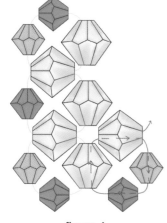

figure 4

Supplies

Large
7 6 mm bicones
8 4 mm bicones, color A
4 4 mm bicones, color B
2 3 mm bicones
6 3 mm pearls
4 2 mm round beads or 11º
seed beads

Small
7 4 mm bicones
8 3 mm bicones, color A
4 3 mm bicones, color B
8 2 mm round crystals
4 2 mm round beads or 11º
seed beads

Both
FireLine, 4-lb. test
needles, size 12
scissors
thread burner

NOTE: For the small component, substitute 4 mm bicones for 6 mm bicones, 3 mm bicones for 4 mm bicones, 2 mm round crystals for 3 mm bicones, and 2 mm round crystals or beads for 3 mm pearls. Use 2 mm round beads or 11º seed beads at the top and bottom.

1. Cut a comfortable length of thread and thread a needle.

2. Pick up one color A 4 mm bicone, one color B 4 mm bicone, and two 6 mm bicones. Slide the beads down the thread, leaving a 6–8-in. (15–20 cm) tail. Pass the needle up through the color A 4 mm bicone to pull the beads together **[figure 1]**. Reinforce, exiting the first 6 mm bicone.

3. Pick up two 6 mm bicones and one color A 4 mm bicone. Pass the needle back through the other side of the first 6 mm bicone **[figure 2]**. Reinforce, exiting the fourth 6 mm bicone.

4. Pick up one color B 4 mm bicone, one color A 4 mm bicone, and one 6 mm bicone. Pass the needle back through the other side of the fourth 6 mm bicone **[figure 3]**. Reinforce, exiting the fifth 6 mm bicone.

5. Pick up one 6 mm bicone, one color B 4 mm bicone, and one color A 4 mm bicone. Pass the needle back up through the fifth 6 mm bicone **[figure 4]**. Reinforce, exiting the sixth 6 mm bicone.

figure 5   figure 6   figure 7

figure 8   figure 9   figure 10

6. Pick up one color A 4 mm bicone and one 6 mm bicone. Pass the needle through the third 6 mm bicone and on through the sixth 6 mm bicone **[figure 5]**. Reinforce, exiting the seventh 6 mm bicone.

7. Pass the needle up through the first 6 mm bicone. Pick up one color A 4 mm bicone and one color B 4 mm bicone. Pass the needle back through the seventh 6 mm bicone **[figure 6]**. Reinforce, exiting the bottom of the color B 4 mm bicone on the right side.

8. Pick up a 3 mm pearl. Pass the needle down through the color A 4 mm bicone. Pick up another 3 mm pearl and continue to pass the needle down through the next two 4 mm bicones **[figure 7]**.

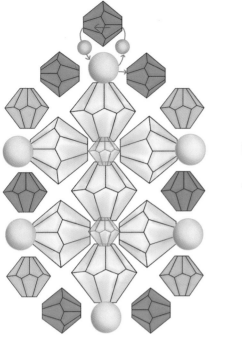

figure 11

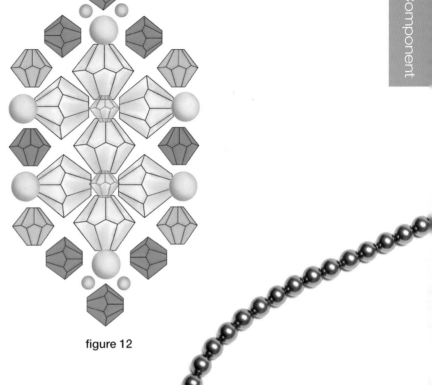

figure 12

9. Pass the needle up through the center 6 mm bicones, adding a 3 mm bicone in between them **[figure 8]**.

10. Repeat step 8 on the left side **[figure 9]**. Pass the needle back up the center, through the 6 mm and 3 mm bicones.

11. Pick up a 3 mm pearl, pass the needle through the outside 4 mm bicones and 3 mm pearls, pick up a 3 mm pearl, and pass through the other outside 4 mm bicones and 3 mm pearls **[figure 10]**. Reinforce, exiting the top 3 mm pearl.

12. Pick up one 2 mm round bead or 11º seed bead, one color A 4 mm bicone, and one 2 mm round bead or 11º. Pass the needle back through the 3 mm pearl **[figure 11]**. Reinforce, passing the needle through the center beads.

13. Repeat step 12 on the bottom **[figure 12]**. Reinforce.

Tudor Romance

Projects

To finish the jewelry shown for this component, turn to Pearl Drop Earrings, p. 60, Drop Pendant, p. 66, Linked Bracelet, p. 63, or Centerpiece Ring, p. 92

The ornate styles and large gemstones in the Showtime TV series *The Tudors* inspired this design. This is how I imagine jewelry from that time period would look—but with a modern twist!

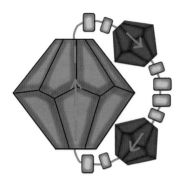

figure 1

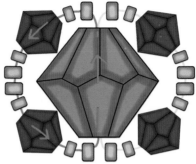

figure 2

Supplies

Large
8 mm bicone, color A
4 4 mm bicones, color B
4 3 mm bicones, color A, or
    4 4 mm bicones, color A
11º seed beads
15º seed beads

Small
6 mm bicone, color A
4 3 mm bicones, color A
4 3 mm bicones, color B
15º seed beads

Both
11º seed beads
15º seed beads
FireLine, 4-lb. test
needles, size 12
scissors
thread burner

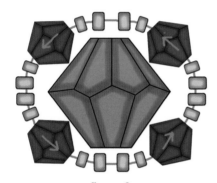

figure 3

NOTE: For the small component, substitute a 6 mm bicone for a 8 mm bicone, 3 mm bicones for 4 mm bicones, and 15º seed beads for 11º seed beads. You may also substitute 4 mm pearls for 4 mm bicones.

1. Cut about 1 yd. (.9 m) of thread and thread a needle.

2. Pick up an 8 mm bicone and slide it down the thread, leaving a 6–8-in. (15–20 cm) tail.

3. Pick up one 11º seed bead, one 15º seed bead, one 4 mm bicone, one 15º, two 11ºs, one 15º, one 4 mm bicone, one 15º, and one 11º. Pass the needle up through the bottom of the 8 mm bicone **[figure 1]**. Reinforce. Repeat step 3 on the other side of the 8 mm bicone **[figure 2]**. Reinforce.

4. Pass the needle through the outside beads surrounding the 8 mm bicone **[figure 3]**. Repeat a few times to pull the beads together, exiting one of the 15ºs.

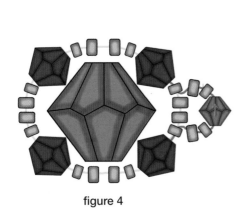

figure 4

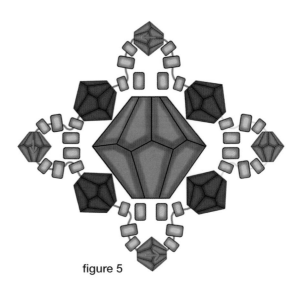

figure 5

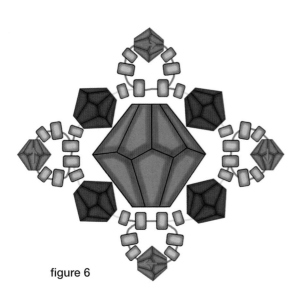

figure 6

5. Pick up one 11º, one 15º, one 3 mm bicone (you may substitute a 4 mm bicone if you wish), one 15º, and one 11º. Pass the needle through the next 15º, 4 mm bicone, and 15º [**figure 4**].

6. Repeat step 5 three more times around the design [**figure 5**].

7. To help the sides hold their shape better, reinforce in this order: Pass the needle through two side 11ºs, then through the next 11º, 15º, and 11º.

8. Complete the circle by passing the needle back through the two 11ºs and [**figure 6**]. Repeat for each side.

Victorian

I love jewelry from the Victorian era of the 1800s. The style is very ornate and colorful. This simple and quick design still looks intricate and delicate.

Projects
To finish the jewelry shown for this component, turn to Simply Pearls, p. 58, Pearl Drop Earrings, p. 60, Drop Pendant, p. 66, or Centerpiece Ring, p. 92

Supplies

Small

4 4 mm bicones, color A
4 4 mm bicones, color B
12 3 mm bicones

Large

4 6 mm bicones, color A
4 6 mm bicones, color B
12 4 mm bicones

Both

11º seed beads
15º seed beads
FireLine, 4-lb. test
needles, size 12
scissors
thread burner

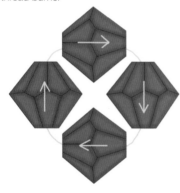

figure 1

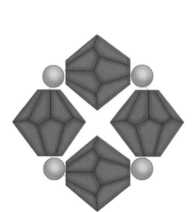

figure 2

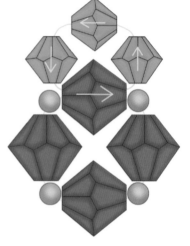

figure 3

NOTE: For the large component, substitute 6 mm bicones for 4 mm bicones and 4 mm bicones for 3 mm bicones.

1. Cut about 38 in. (.97 m) of thread and thread a needle. Pick up four color A 4 mm bicones.

2. Slide the beads down the thread, leaving about an 8-in. (20 cm) tail. Pass the needle back through the beads, starting with the first bicone you picked up. Pull the circle of bicones closed **[figure 1]**.

3. Pass the needle back through the 4 mm bicones again, but this time add an 11º seed bead in between

each one **[figure 2]**. Exit a 4 mm bicone.

4. Pick up three 3 mm bicones and pass the needle back through the other end of the 4 mm bicone **[figure 3]**. Reinforce.

NOTE: Make sure you are always exiting a crystal or going directly into one. Do not accidentally go through any 11ºs in this step.

5. Repeat step 4 three more times around the design **[figure 4]**.

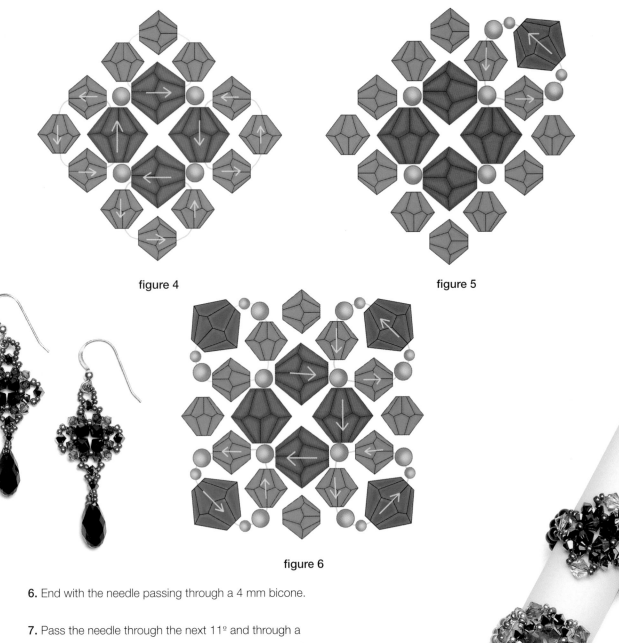

figure 4

figure 5

figure 6

6. End with the needle passing through a 4 mm bicone.

7. Pass the needle through the next 11º and through a 3 mm bicone **[figure 5]**. Pick up one 11º, one 15º seed bead, one color B 4 mm bicone, one 15º, and one 11º. Pass the needle through the 3 mm bicone to the left of the one you are currently exiting. Reinforce.

8. Repeat steps 7 and 8 three more times around the design. Reinforce as you go **[figure 6]**.

Butterfly

I love the versatility of this design. It shimmers in soft pastels, but the colors really pop when you use bold colors. Also, the seed beads in this design play a dominant role in helping your beautiful crystals stand out. The sky's the limit!

Projects
To finish the jewelry shown for this component, turn to Chain Necklace, p. 56, or Centerpiece Ring, p. 92.

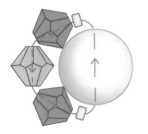

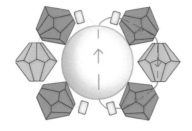

figure 1

figure 2

Supplies
2 6 mm bicones, color A
6 4 mm bicones, color A
6 4 mm bicones, color B
6 3 mm bicones, color B
6 mm pearl
3 mm pearl
15º seed beads
11º seed beads
FireLine, 4-lb. test
needle, size 12
scissors
thread burner

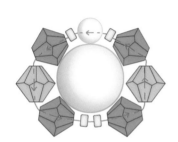

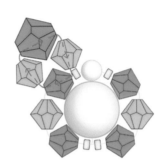

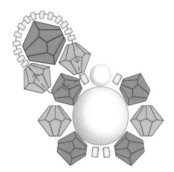

figure 3

figure 4

figure 5

1. Cut about 40 in. (1 m) of thread and thread a needle.

2. Pick up one 6 mm pearl and slide it down the thread, leaving an 8-in. (20 cm) tail.

3. Pick up one 11º seed bead, one color A 4 mm bicone, one color B 4 mm bicone, one color A 4 mm bicone, and one 11º. Pass the needle back up through the 6 mm pearl **[figure 1]**. Reinforce.

4. Repeat step 3 on the other side of the 6 mm pearl **[figure 2]**.

5. Passing the needle through the beads surrounding the 6 mm pearl, pull together the bottom 11ºs, and add a

3 mm pearl in between the top two 11ºs **[figure 3]**. Reinforce, exiting the top-left color A 4 mm bicone from the left side.

6. Pick up one color B 4 mm bicone, one color A 6 mm bicone, and one color B 4 mm bicone. Pass the needle back through the 4 mm bicone **[figure 4]**. Reinforce, exiting the first color B 4 mm bicone you just added.

7. Pick up 14 15º seed beads. Pass the needle down through the other color B 4 mm bicone and the top-left color A 4 mm bicone **[figure 5]**. Reinforce.

8. With the needle exiting the bottom-left color A 4 mm bicone, pick up one color B 3 mm bicone, one color A

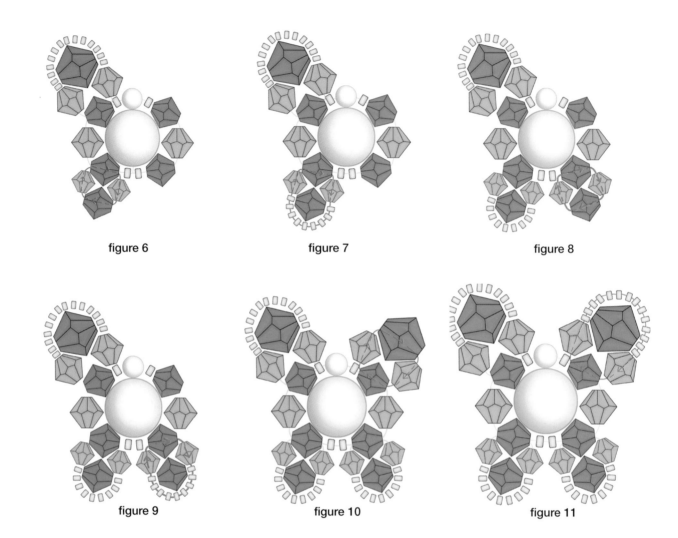

figure 6

figure 7

figure 8

figure 9

figure 10

figure 11

4 mm bicone, and one color B 3 mm bicone. Pass the needle back through the other side of the bottom-left color A 4 mm bicone **[figure 6]**. Reinforce, exiting the first color B 3 mm bicone you just added.

9. Pick up nine 15°s. Pass the needle through the other color B 3 mm bicone and the bottom-left color A 4 mm bicone **[figure 7]**. Reinforce.

10. Repeat steps 8 and 9 on the bottom-right of the design, exiting the top-right color A 4 mm bicone **[figures 8 and 9]**.

11. Repeat steps 6 and 7 **[figures 10 and 11]**. Exit the 3 mm pearl from the left side.

12. Pick up five 15°s. Pass the needle down through the nearest color B 4 mm bicone **[figure 12]**.

13. Pass the needle back through the 3 mm pearl so it is exiting the right side. Pick up five 15°s. Pass the needle down through the nearest color B 4 mm bicone, exiting the remaining color B 4 mm bicone on the top-left wing **[figure 13]**.

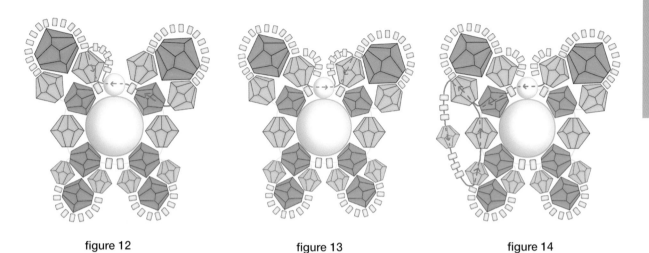

figure 12

figure 13

figure 14

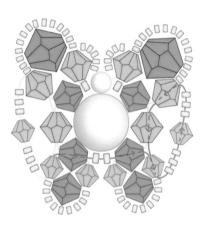

figure 15

Try something different

Embellish the butterfly as you like. Add loops of seed beads to the wings, or use cubic zirconia drops for even more glitter.

14. Pick up three 15ºs, one color B 3 mm bicone, and three 15ºs. Pass the needle through the nearest 3 mm bicone on the bottom-left wing and the color B 4 mm bicone between the wings **[figure 14]**. Reinforce.

15. Repeat step 14 on the right side of the design **[figure 15]**. Reinforce.

Fairy Flower

Projects

To finish the jewelry shown for this component, turn to Simply Pearls, p. 58, Pearl Drop Earrings, p. 60, or Centerpiece Ring, p. 92.

I am always playing around with my crystals to find new ways of putting them together. This whimsical design was a happy accident. The Fairy Flower looks absolutely lovely in many different colors— try making blooms to match any outfit in your wardrobe!

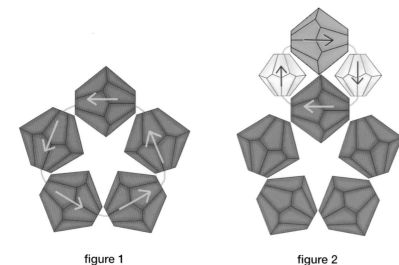

figure 1

figure 2

Supplies

Small
5 4 mm bicones, color A
5 4 mm bicones, color B
10 3 mm bicones, color C
10 3 mm bicones, color D
15º seed beads

Large
5 6 mm bicone, color A
5 6 mm bicones, color B
10 4 mm bicones, color C
10 4 mm bicones, color D
11º seed beads

Both
FireLine, 4-lb. test
needles, size 12
scissors
thread burner

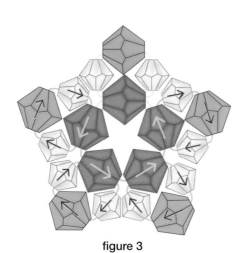

figure 3

NOTE: To make the large component, substitute
6 mm bicones for 4 mm bicones, 4 mm bicones for
3 mm bicones, and 11º seed beads for 15º seed beads.

1. Cut a comfortable length of thread and thread a needle.

2. Pick up five color A 4 mm bicones. Slide them down
the thread, leaving an 8-in. (20 cm) tail. Pass the needle
back through the bicones, beginning with the first one

picked up [**figure 1**]. Reinforce, exiting one of the color A
4 mm bicones.

3. Pick up one color C 3 mm bicone, one color B 4 mm
bicone, and one color C 3 mm bicone. Pass the needle
back through the other side of the color A 4 mm bicone
[**figure 2**]. Reinforce.

4. Repeat step 3 four more times around the design,
exiting a color C 3 mm bicone [**figure 3**].

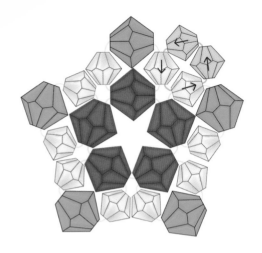

figure 4

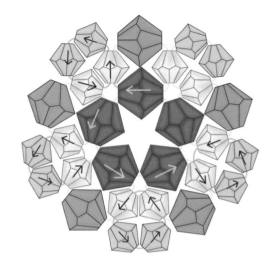

figure 5

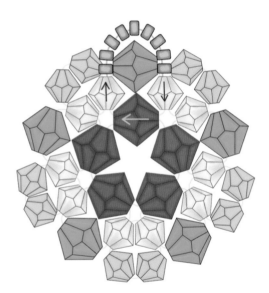

figure 6

figure 7

5. Pick up two color D 3 mm bicones. Pass the needle down through the color C 3 mm bicone next to the one you started with **[figure 4]**. Reinforce, going only through the 3 mm bicones.

6. Repeat step 5 four more times around the design **[figure 5]**. Exit a color C 3 mm bicone.

7. Pick up nine 15º seed beads. Pass the needle down through the color C 3 mm bicone on the other side of the nearest color B 4 mm bicone, then go through the color A 4 mm bicone below the color B 4 mm bicone **[figure 6]**. Reinforce.

8. Repeat step 7 four more times around the design **[figure 7]**.

figure 8

9. Add a 15º seed bead in between each of the color A
4 mm bicones **[figure 8]**.

Snowflake

Projects
To finish the jewelry shown for this component, turn to Chain Necklace, p. 56, Drop Pendant, p. 66, or Centerpiece Ring, p. 92.

Watching the seasons change is part of the joy of living up north. I lived in Florida for a few years and I missed the brisk winter air, but playing around with colors like opal, ice, and light blue kept me cool in a warm climate.

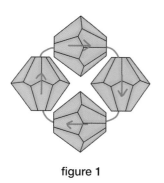

figure 1

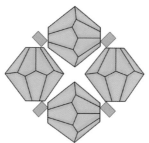

figure 2

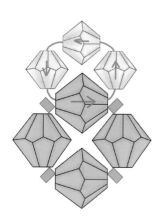

figure 3

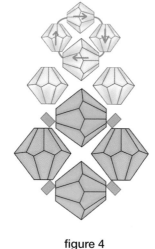

figure 4

Supplies

Small
8 4 mm bicones
24 3 mm bicones
24 2.5 mm bicones
11º seed beads
15º seed beads

Large
8 6 mm bicones
24 4 mm bicones
24 3 mm bicones
11º seed beads

Both
FireLine, 4-lb. or 6-lb. test
needle, size 12
scissors
thread burner

NOTE: To make the large component, substitute 6 mm bicones for 4 mm bicones, 4 mm bicones for 3 mm bicones, 3 mm bicones for 2.5 mm bicones, and 11º seed beads for 15º seed beads.

1. Cut a comfortable length of thread and thread a needle.

2. Pick up four 4 mm bicones. Slide them down thread, leaving about an 8-in. (20 cm) tail. Pass the needle back up through the beads, starting with the first 4 mm bicone you picked up **[figure 1]**. Reinforce, adding an 11º seed

bead in between the 4 mm bicones **[figure 2]**. Exit one of the 4 mm bicones.

3. Pick up three 3 mm bicones. Pass the needle back through the other side of the 4 mm bicone **[figure 3]**. Reinforce, exiting the top center 3 mm bicone.

4. Pick up three 2.5 mm bicones. Pass the needle back through the other side of the 3 mm bicone **[figure 4]**. Reinforce, exiting the top center 2.5 mm bicone.

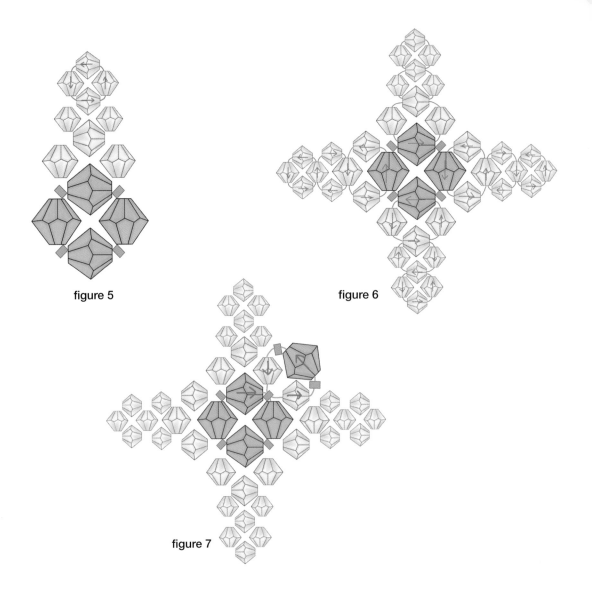

figure 5

figure 6

figure 7

5. Pick up three more 2.5 mm bicones. Pass the needle back through the other side of the bottom 2.5 mm bicone **[figure 5]**. Reinforce.

NOTE: Be sure to reinforce the thread several times, or you will have a droopy snowflake.

6. Repeat steps 3–5 three more times around the design **[figure 6]**. Exit one of the 3 mm bicones.

7. Pick up one 15º seed bead, one 4 mm bicone, and one 15º. Pass the needle down through the nearest 3 mm bicone **[figure 7]**. Reinforce, exiting the 4 mm bicone you just added.

8. Pick up three 3 mm bicones. Pass the needle back through the other side of the 4 mm bicone **[figure 8]**. Reinforce.

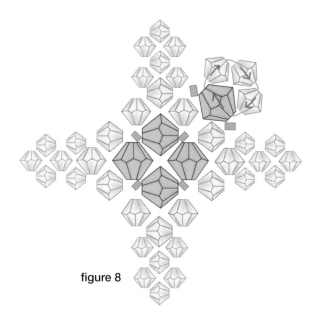

figure 8

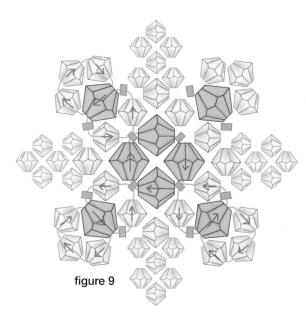

figure 9

9. Repeat steps 7 and 8 three more times around the design [**figure 9**]. Reinforce.

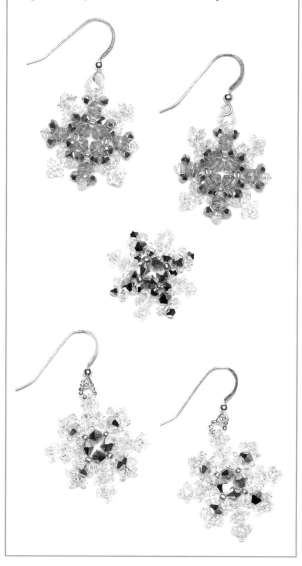

Try something different

The Snowflake design works well with several icy color palettes. Choose Swarovski crystals in Turquoise AB2X, Crystal, Crystal AB, Crystal AB2X, Aquamarine AB2X, Light Azore AB2X, Sky Blue Opal, White Opal, Comet Argent Light, or Crystal CAL AB for a frosty look.

Royal Beauty

When I think of portraits of royalty from the 1500s, I think of colorful, romantic pieces. I love the pearls incorporated into this base design. They give the piece a regal feel while still allowing plenty of room for sparkly crystals! A queen would feel right at home with this set.

Projects

To finish the jewelry shown for this component, turn to Pearl Drop Earrings, p. 60, Drop Pendant, p. 66, or Centerpiece Ring, p. 92.

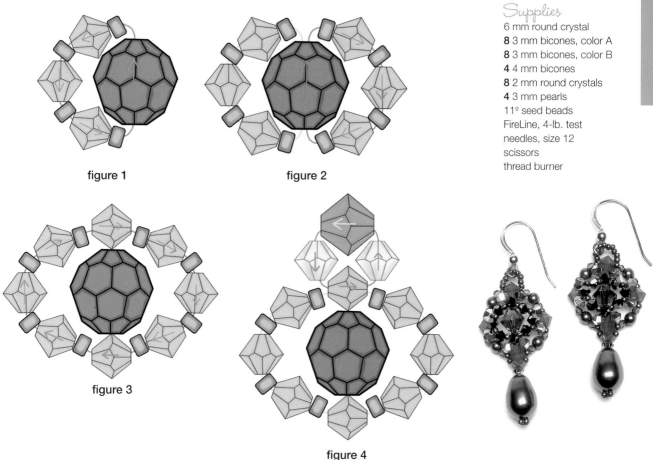

figure 1

figure 2

figure 3

figure 4

Supplies

6 mm round crystal
8 3 mm bicones, color A
8 3 mm bicones, color B
4 4 mm bicones
8 2 mm round crystals
4 3 mm pearls
11º seed beads
FireLine, 4-lb. test
needles, size 12
scissors
thread burner

1. Cut a comfortable length of thread and thread a needle.

2. Pick up one 6 mm round crystal, one 11º seed bead, one color A 3 mm bicone, one 11º, one color A 3 mm bicone, one 11º seed bead, one color A 3 mm bicone, and one 11º. Slide them down the thread, leaving an 8–10-in. (20–25 cm) tail.

3. Pass the needle back through the 6 mm round, and pull the other beads against it **[figure 1]**. Reinforce.

4. Repeat steps 2 and 3 (skipping the 6 mm round) on the other side of the 6 mm round **[figure 2]**. Reinforce.

5. Pick up a color A 3 mm bicone and pass through the next 11º, 3 mm bicone, 11º, 3 mm bicone, 11º, 3 mm bicone, and 11º. Pick up another color A 3 mm bicone, and continue through the remaining 11ºs and bicones surrounding the 6 mm round **[figure 3]**. Reinforce, exiting the top 3 mm bicone.

6. Pick up one color B 3 mm bicone, one 4 mm bicone, and one color B 3 mm bicone. Pass the needle through the other side of the top color A 3 mm bicone **[figure 4]**. Reinforce.

figure 5

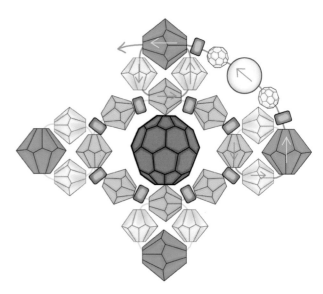

figure 6

7. Skip the next color A 3 mm bicone, and go through the next. Repeat step 6. Reinforce. Repeat twice more around the design, exiting one of the 4 mm bicones **[figure 5]**.

8. Pick up one 11º seed bead, one 2 mm round crystal, one 3 mm pearl, one 2 mm round crystal, and one 11º. Pass the needle through the next 4 mm bicone. To secure this step, pass the needle through the color B 3 mm bicone, through the color A 3 mm bicone, back up through the other color B 3 mm bicone, and back through the 4 mm bicone **[figure 6]**.

9. Repeat step 8 three more times around the design **[figure 7]**. Reinforce.

figure 7

Rosette

Projects

To finish the jewelry shown for this component, turn to Simply Pearls, p. 58, Pearl Drop Earrings, p. 60, or Centerpiece Ring, p 92.

Take it up a notch and make a three-dimensional design. This medallion-style piece covered with delicious crystals is truly a one-of-a-kind showstopper, perfect for a fancy evening out on the town.

figure 1

figure 2

figure 3

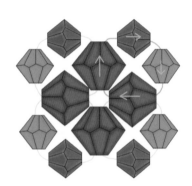

figure 4

NOTE: To make the small component, substitute 6 mm bicones for 8 mm bicones and 4 mm bicones for 6 mm bicones.

1. Cut a comfortable length of thread and thread a needle.

2. Pick up two 8 mm bicones, one color A 6 mm bicone, and one color B 6 mm bicone. Pass the needle back up through these beads, starting with the first 8 mm bicone you picked up. Pull together and reinforce **[figure 1]**. Exit the bottom 8 mm bicone.

3. Pick up one 8 mm bicone, one color A 6 mm bicone, and one color B 6 mm bicone. Pass the needle through the other side of the first 8 mm bicone in this step **[figure 2]**. Reinforce, exiting the bottom of the 8 mm bicone.

4. Pick up one color A 6 mm bicone, one color B 6 mm bicone, and one 8 mm bicone. Pass the needle back down through the 8 mm bicone you started with **[figure 3]**. Reinforce, exiting the 8 mm bicone just added.

5. Pass the needle up through the top 8 mm bicone. Pick up one color A 6 mm bicone and one color B 6 mm bicone **[figure 4]**. Reinforce.

6. Flip the design over. Pick up two 8 mm bicones and pass the needle through the top color A 6 mm bicone **[figure 5]**. Reinforce, exiting the middle 8 mm bicone.

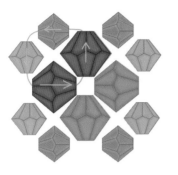

figure 5

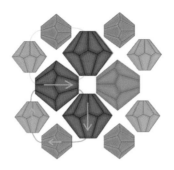

figure 6

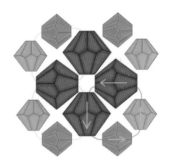

figure 7

figure 8

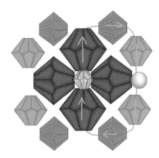

figure 9

7. Pick up another 8 mm bicone and pass the needle through the bottom color A 6 mm bicone **[figure 6]**. Reinforce, exiting the bottom of the 8 mm bicone.

8. Pass the needle through both the color A and B 6 mm bicones. Pick up another 8 mm bicone and pass the needle back down through the 8 mm bicone you started with in this step **[figure 7]**. Reinforce, exiting the 8 mm bicone on the right side.

9. Pass the needle up through the top 8 mm bicone. Continue and pass the needle through the 6 mm bicones on the top right side **[figure 8]**. Reinforce, exiting the color B 6 mm bicone on the right side.

10. Pick up a 3 mm pearl. Continue passing through the remaining 6 mm bicones on the right side.

11. Pass the needle up through the bottom 8 mm bicone. Pick up a 3 mm bicone (you may also use a 4 mm bicone), and continue through the top 8 mm bicone **[figure 9]**. Reinforce.

12. Flip the design back over. (The 3 mm pearl will now be on the left side.) Pass the needle through the two 6 mm bicones on the right side.

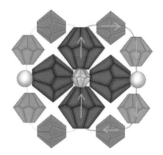

figure 10

13. Pick up a 3 mm pearl. Continue passing through the remaining 6 mm bicones on the right side. Pass the needle up through the bottom 8 mm bicone. Pick up a 3 mm bicone and continue through the top 8 mm bicone **[figure 10]**. Reinforce. (You will have a pearl on both sides and a 3 mm bicone on the front and back.)

14. Pass the needle around the outside perimeter, adding a 3 mm pearl on the bottom and top **[figure 11]** (see "Try something different" to string this component on beading wire).

15. Weave in any excess thread and trim.

figure 11

Try something different

To string this design on beading wire, slide the wire through the top 6 mm bicone on one side and then string the 3 mm pearl. Next, pass the beading wire through to the 6 mm bicone on the other side. If you wait until the very end to string, it will be difficult to get the beading wire through the pearl.

Bouquet

Projects
To finish the jewelry shown for this component, turn to Peyote Pendant, p. 88, or Centerpiece Ring, p. 92

If crystals and seed beads aren't enough, add a little more flash with flower sequins. This spin-off of the Rosette design was born when my local bead shop got sequins in for the first time. Because they sparkle, I naturally had to find a use for them.

Supplies

8 8 mm bicones
8 6 mm bicones
2 mm round crystal
11º seed beads
9 6 mm cupped flower
  sequins
FireLine, 4-lb. test
needle, size 12
scissors
thread burner

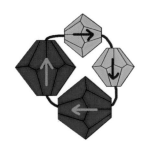

figure 1

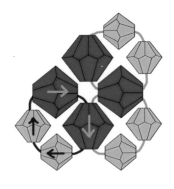

figure 2

figure 3

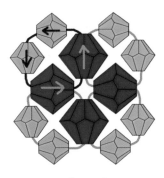

figure 4

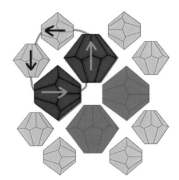

figure 5

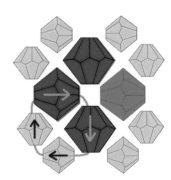

figure 6

1. Cut a comfortable length of thread, and thread a needle. Create the "Rosette" base design on page 43 without the pearls **[figures 1–7]**. Exit between two corner 6 mm bicones.

2. You will be adding the sequins just to the front of the design. Pick up one sequin and one 11º seed bead. Pass the needle back down through the sequin and slide the sequin down the thread to make sure that it will be tight against the design. Pass the needle up through the adjacent 8 mm bicone **[figure 8]**. Reinforce.

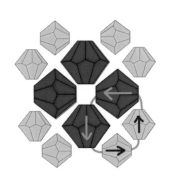

figure 7

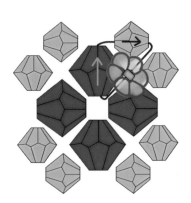

figure 8

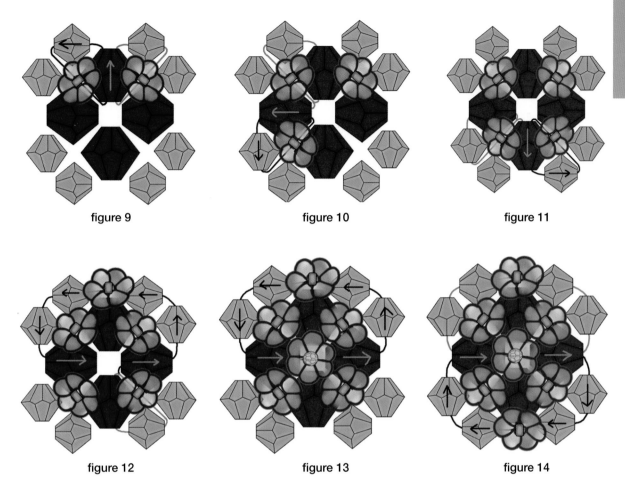

figure 9   figure 10   figure 11

figure 12   figure 13   figure 14

3. Repeat step 2 three more times around the design [**figures 9–11**]. Reinforce as you go, and exit the top-right corner 6 mm bicones.

4. Add a sequin and go through the top-left 6 mm bicones and the left 8 mm bicone [**figure 12**].

5. Add a center sequin, but use a 2 mm round crystal instead of an 11º [**figure 13**]. Pass the needle through the right 8 mm bicone and the side sequin added in step 4 to reinforce.

6. Repeat step 5 on the bottom of the design [**figure 14**]. Reinforce by passing back through the center sequin.

7. To add the final two sequins, pass the needle through the outside 6 mm bicones and sequins, adding a sequin in between the side 6 mm bicones [**figures 15 and 16**].

8. Still passing the needle through the outside 6 mm bicones and sequins, add an 11º under each of the side sequins [**figure 17**]. This will boost up the sequins.

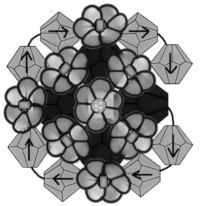

figure 15

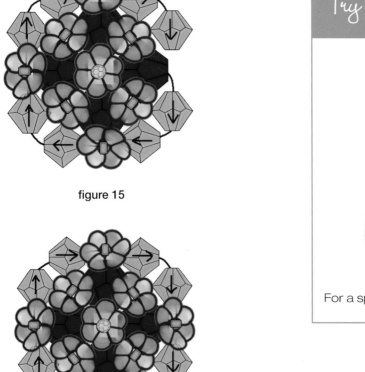

figure 16

Try something different

For a sparkly ball, add sequins on both sides.

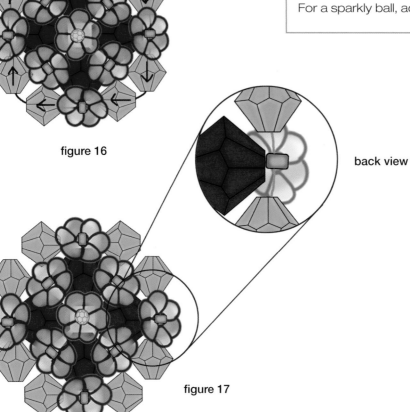

back view

figure 17

Enchanted Star

Projects

To finish the jewelry shown for this component, turn to Pearl Drop Earrings, p. 60. Crystal Link Bracelet, p. 72, or Centerpiece Ring, p. 92.

Weave a midnight fantasy in sparkling crystals. Whether you like dramatic, wintery nights or a warm summer evening, this enchanted star will glitter and shine.

6 mm bicone
10 3 mm bicones, color A
20 3 mm bicones, color B
FireLine, 4-lb. test
needle, size 12
scissors
thread burner

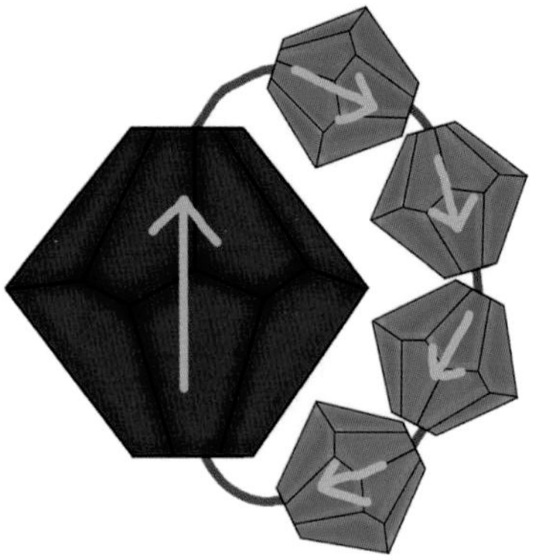

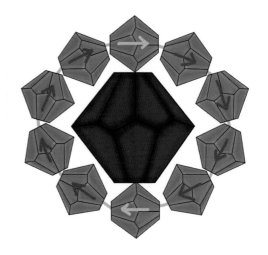

figure 1

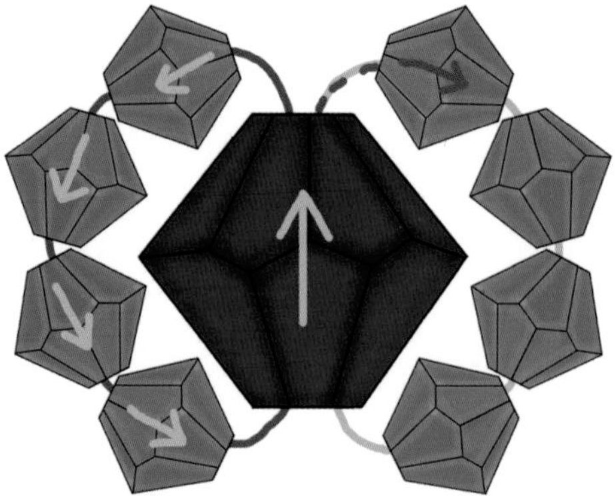

figure 2

1. Cut a comfortable length of thread and thread a needle. Pick up one 6 mm bicone and four color A 3 mm bicones. Pass the needle back up through the 6 mm bicone **[figure 1]**. Reinforce.

2. Pick up four color A 3 mm bicones, and pass the needle back through the 6 mm bicone **[figure 2]**. Reinforce.

3. Pick up a color A 3 mm bicone and pass the needle through the next four 3 mm bicones. Pick up a color A 3 mm bicone, continue through the remaining 3 mm

figure 3

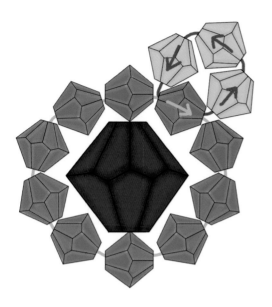

figure 4

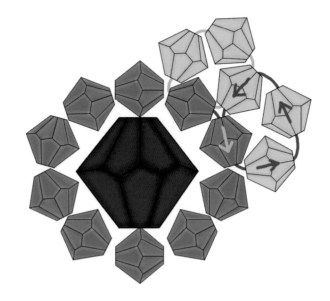

figure 5

bicones **[figure 3]**. Reinforce, exiting one of the 3 mm bicones.

4. Pick up three color B 3 mm bicones and pass the needle back through that same 3 mm bicone **[figure 4]**. Reinforce.

5. Pass the needle through the next color A 3 mm bicone. Pick up two color B 3 mm bicones and pass the needle down through the first 3 mm bicone from the previous step **[figure 5]**. Reinforce.

6. Repeat step 5 around the design until complete **[figure 6]**. You will only add one color B 3 mm bicone in the last repeat. Reinforce as you go.

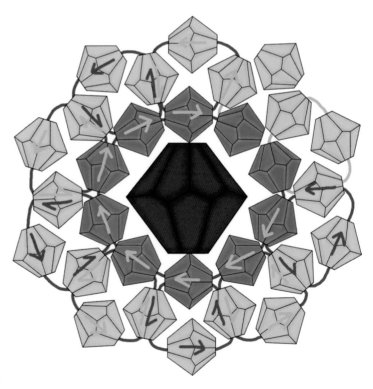

figure 6

Finished

Jewelry

Once you've created your crystal components, flip through this section to choose a finished jewelry piece. Whether you want a necklace, bracelet, pair of earrings, ring, or even a headband, you'll find plenty to tempt you!

Chain Necklace

A perfect setting for the Butterfly, Tudor Romance, or Snowflake component, a simple chain is fast and easy.

Supplies
1 crystal component
4 5–7 mm jump rings
16–20 in. (41–51 cm) chain
clasp
2 pairs of chainnose pliers
wire cutters
needles, size 12
thread burner

1. End the working thread and tail on the component.

2. Decide how long you want your necklace to be and divide the length in half. Cut two pieces of chain to that length.

3. Open a jump ring and slip it through one end link of chain and one side of the component. Close the jump ring **[figure]**. Attach half of the clasp to the other end of the chain.

4. Repeat step 2 with the other chain length.

Try something different

Connect a few different components and use cord crimp ends to attach a cord instead of chain. You will have to add the cord crimp ends to the top while you are making the component.

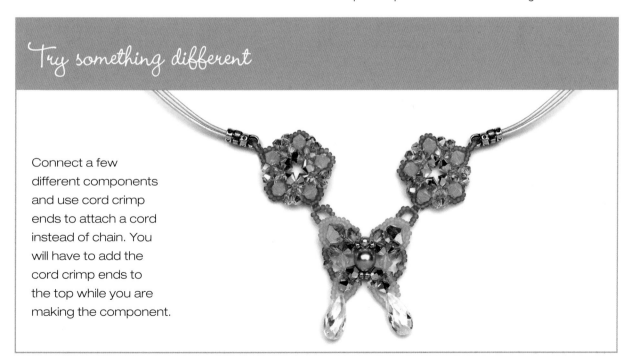

57

Simply Pearls

For a quick
and easy piece,
string pearls with
any component
in this book. Feel
free to try other
beautiful beads
to complement
your crystals
as well!

Supplies

1 component
16-in. (41 cm) strand
  6 mm pearls
4 4 mm pearls
clasp
2 crimp beads
2 crimp covers (optional)
flexible beading wire, .019
needle, size 12
thread burner
crimping pliers
chainnose pliers
wire cutters

1. Decide how long you want your necklace to be. Cut a piece of beading wire to that length plus a few inches.

2. Slide the beading wire through one of (or several of) the bicones at the top of the component. String 6 mm pearls on both sides of the component **[figure]**, ending with two 4 mm pearls. Add a few crystal accents as well, if you like.

3. On one end, string a crimp bead and half of the clasp, and go back through the crimp bead and a few more beads. Check the fit, and add or remove beads as necessary. Crimp the crimp bead and trim any excess wire. Cover the crimp, if desired.

4. Repeat step 3 on the other end of the necklace.

5. End the working thread and tail on the component.

Try something different

For a component with large loops on the sides, like the Butterfly, cut a length of beading wire and string a crimp bead and a loop of the component. Crimp the crimp bead, then string seed beads, pearls, cubic zirconia drops, and crystals until you reach the desired length. Repeat on the other side of the component. Finish as in main project.

Pearl Drop Earrings

Adding just a pearl makes any design instantly elegant. Explore the possibilities with Fairy Flower, Heirloom, Royal Beauty, Tudor Romance, or Snowflake components.

Supplies

2 components
mix of 15º seed beads,
    2 mm round crystals, or
    2 mm pearls
2 8 x 11 mm pearl drops
pair of earring findings
FireLine, 4-lb. test
needle, size 12
thread burner
2 pairs of chainnose pliers

1. Using the working thread or 6–8-in. (15–20 cm) tail (whichever is longest), exit a bicone on the bottom of the component. Pick up 2–4 15º seed beads, crystals, or pearls. Pick up one pearl drop, and two 15ºs.

2. Pass the needle back up through the pearl drop and first bead above the drop. Pick 2–4 15º seed beads, crystals, or pearls, crystals, or pearls **[figure]**. Reinforce.

3. Weave the needle to the top of the component so it exits a bicone.

4. Pick up 6–10 15ºs. Pass the needle back through the other side of the bicone. Reinforce.

5. End the working thread and tail.

6. Open the loop of an earring finding, slide it through the loop made in step 4, and close the loop **[figure]**.

7. Repeat to make a second earring.

The amount of seed beads you use to attach the drops and earring findings will change the length and look of the piece. If you like, use 11º seed beads instead of 15º s, but use fewer. Space 2 mm round crystals between the seed beads for even more sparkle.

Use a crystal or glass dangle instead of a pearl.

Simply add an ear wire to a loop.

Linked Bracelet

Join components into a
chain of crystals. The Keepsake
and Snowflake designs make
especially lovely links.

Supplies

7–8 components
6–7 4 mm bicones
11° seed beads
clasp
FireLine, 4-lb. test
needles, size 12
scissors
thread burner

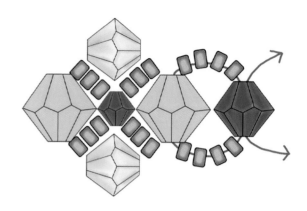

figure 1

1. Cut a comfortable length of thread and thread a needle on both ends. Pass a needle through an end bicone on one component, centering the component on the thread.

2. Pick up four 11° seed beads on each needle, and then pass both needles through a 4 mm bicone in opposite directions **[figure 1]**. Pick up four 11°s on each needle **[figure 2]**.

3. Pass both needles through an end bicone on another component, going in opposite directions **[figure 3]**. Weave through the component to exit the end bicone on the opposite side.

4. Repeat steps 2 and 3, continuing until you have reached the desired length. With one needle, exit an end bicone.

5. Pick up eleven 11°s and half of the clasp. Pass the needle back through the end bicone from the other side **[figure 4]**. Reinforce.

6. Using a working thread from a component on the opposite end of the bracelet, repeat step 5.

7. End all the threads.

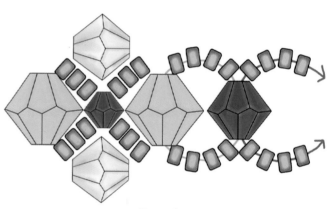

figure 2

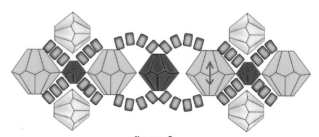

figure 3

Try something different

Add either bicones (pictured), round crystals, or pearls between the linking seed beads in the center.

figure 4

Try something different

You can connect some components with only a few seed beads.

Drop Pendant

Add a drop of class to the Heirloom, Rosette, Royal Beauty, Tudor Romance, or Victorian components with a simple pearl. Or, go bare with a wire bail.

Supplies

1 component
mix of 11º seed beads,
    2 mm round crystals, or
    2 mm pearls
3 mm bicone (optional)
8 x 11 mm pearl drop
16-in. (41 cm) strand
    6 mm pearls
clasp
2 crimp beads
2 crimp covers (optional)
flexible beading wire, .019
FireLine, 4-lb. test
needle, size 12
thread burner
chainnose pliers
crimping pliers
wire cutters

Try something different

For a quick pendant without the pearl drops, make a set of wraps and a wrapped loop above a component. Use 24- or 26-gauge wire to make this bail, then slide it on a chain to wear.

1. Using the working thread or 6–8 in. (15–20 cm) tail (whichever is longest), exit a bottom bicone. Pick up 1–2 11º seed beads, 2 mm round crystals, or pearls. Pick up one 3 mm bicone (or another 11º), one pearl drop, and two 11ºs.

2. Pass the needle back through the pearl drop and 3 mm bicone or 11º **[figure]**.

3. Pick up two more 11ºs and pass the needle back through the other side of the 3 mm bicone **[figure]**. Reinforce.

4. Follow the steps for "Simply Pearls," p. 58, to string the pendant and complete the necklace.

Two-drop Earrings

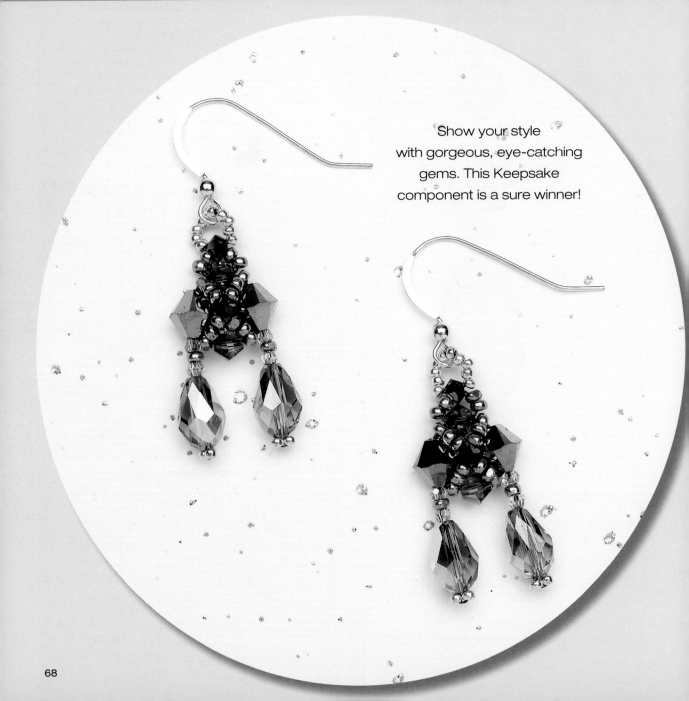

Show your style with gorgeous, eye-catching gems. This Keepsake component is a sure winner!

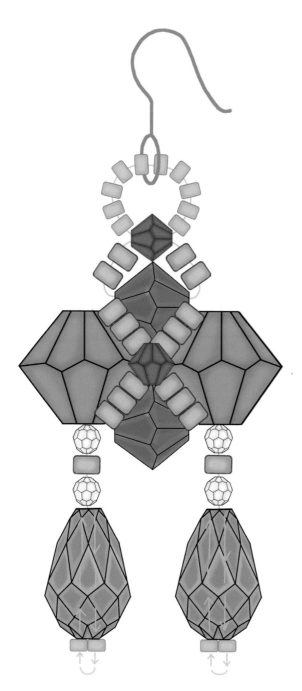

Supplies
2 components
4 9 x 6 mm crystal drops
2 3 mm bicones
8 2 mm round crystals
11º seed beads
15º seed beads
pair of earring findings
FireLine, 4-lb. test
needle, size 12
thread burner
2 pairs of chainnose pliers

1. Using the working tail or 6–8 in. (15–20 cm) tail (whichever is longest), exit a vertical side bicone. Pick up one 2 mm round crystal, one 11º seed bead, one 2 mm round crystal, one crystal drop, and two 15º seed beads **[figure]**.

2. Pass the needle back through the drop, 2 mm round crystals, 11º, and side bicone **[figure]**.

3. Weave the needle to the other side of the component and repeat the previous steps **[figure]**. Then go back through the beads on the first side to reinforce. Repeat on the second side.

4. With the thread exiting a top bicone, pick up 2–4 11ºs, a 3 mm bicone, and 6–10 15ºs. Go back through the 3 mm bicone, pick up 2–4 11ºs, and go through the top bicone from the opposite direction **[figure]**. Reinforce.

5. End the working thread and tail.

6. Open the loop of an earring finding, slide it through the component loop, and close the loop.

7. Repeat to make a second earring.

Stacked Earrings

If one component isn't enough for you, make a couple in different sizes and stack them. The Keepsake component works well, but you can experiment with other sizes and styles to your heart's content.

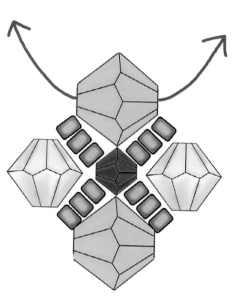

figure 1

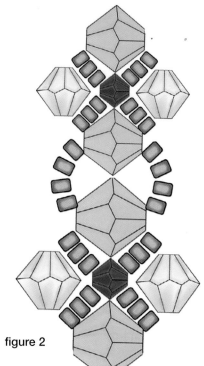

figure 2

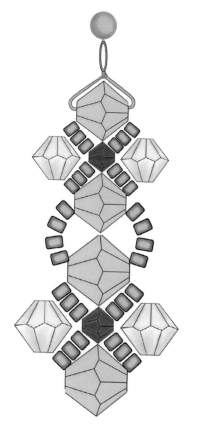

figure 3

Supplies

2 large components
2 small components
11º seed beads
6 in. (15 cm) 24–26-gauge
   wire
pair of earring findings
FireLine, 4-lb. test
needles, size 12
scissors
thread burner
chainnose pliers
roundnose pliers
wire cutters

1. Cut a comfortable length of thread and thread a needle on each end. Center the top horizontal bicone of a large component on the thread **[figure 1]**.

2. Pick up four 11º seed beads on both needles. Pass the needles through the bottom horizontal bicone of the small component, going in opposite directions **[figure 2]**. Reinforce.

3. End all the threads.

4. Cut 3 in. (7.6 cm) of wire and string the top bicone of the small component on the wire **[figure 3]**. Make a set of wraps above the bicone, then make a wrapped loop.

5. Open the loop of an earring finding, slide it through the wrapped loop, and close the loop.

6. Repeat to make a second earring.

What better way to link crystal components than with more crystals? The Tudor Romance and Victorian components show off the possibilities.

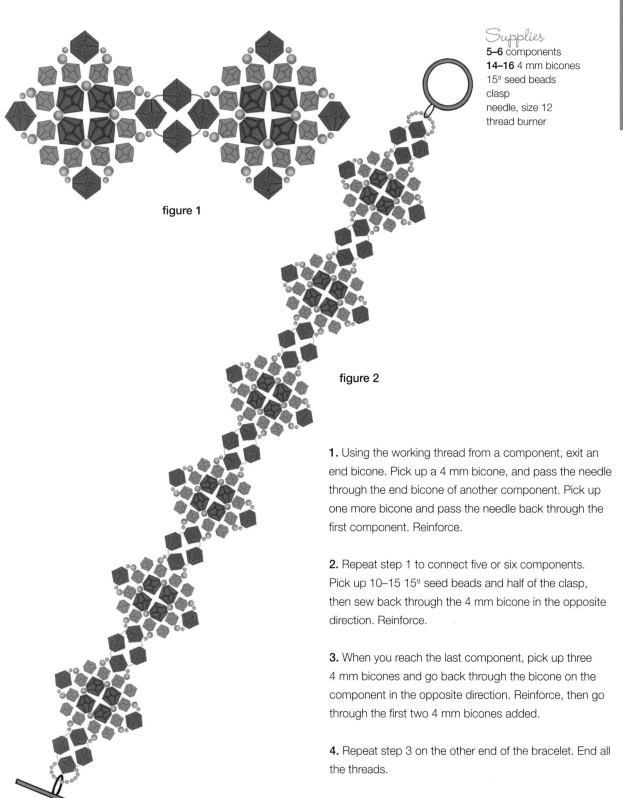

figure 1

figure 2

Supplies
5–6 components
14–16 4 mm bicones
15º seed beads
clasp
needle, size 12
thread burner

1. Using the working thread from a component, exit an end bicone. Pick up a 4 mm bicone, and pass the needle through the end bicone of another component. Pick up one more bicone and pass the needle back through the first component. Reinforce.

2. Repeat step 1 to connect five or six components. Pick up 10–15 15º seed beads and half of the clasp, then sew back through the 4 mm bicone in the opposite direction. Reinforce.

3. When you reach the last component, pick up three 4 mm bicones and go back through the bicone on the component in the opposite direction. Reinforce, then go through the first two 4 mm bicones added.

4. Repeat step 3 on the other end of the bracelet. End all the threads.

Combine two components into one unique style. No need to match—let your imagination wander!

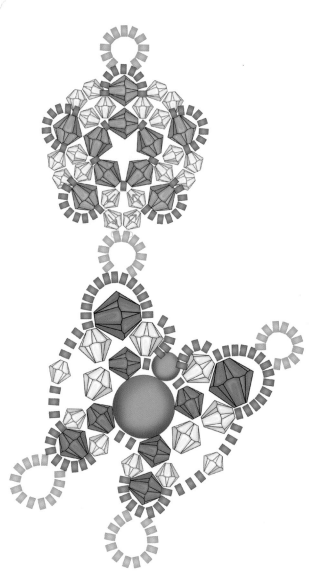

Supplies
4 components, **2** of each style
15º seed beads
pair of earring findings
needle, size 12
thread burner
2 pairs of chainnose pliers

from the second component, exit the top of the component. Pick up 10–12 15º seed beads and go back through the top of the component from the opposite direction. Reinforce.

4. End all the threads.

5. Open the loop of an earring finding, slide it through the loop made in the step 3, and close the loop.

6. Repeat to make a second earring.

1. Using the working thread or 6–8 in. (15–20 cm) tail (whichever is longest), exit the top or top corner of a component.

2. Pick up five or six 15º seed beads and weave through the bottom of a second component so the needle exits adjacent to where it entered. Pick up five or six 15ºs and go through the top of the first component so the needle enters adjacent to where it exited. Reinforce.

3. Using the working thread or 6–8 in. (15–20 cm) tail

Try something different

If you want to combine any of these patterns, there is a way; think about the way the components will hinge, and decide how many seed beads or extra crystals to add. Make all kinds of different connections!

Gypsy Earrings

Pair cubic zirconia drops with Victorian components for cute dangles that look great with a comfy sweater. Choose bright, cheerful colors for casual style, or make a dramatic version in black and white.

figure 1

Supplies

2 components
6 6 x 12 mm faceted cubic
   zirconia pear drop
   briolettes
10 3 mm bicones, color A
20 3 mm bicones, color B
12 2 mm round crystals
11º seed beads
15º seed beads
pair of earwires
FireLine, 4-lb. test
needles, size 12
scissors
thread burner

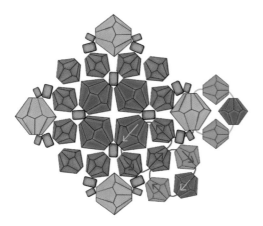

figure 2

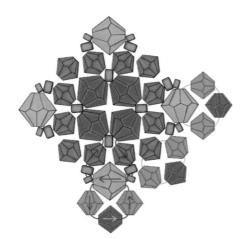

figure 3

NOTE: I used a Victorian component to complete this design. For another component, skip or alter steps 1–5 as needed to embellish these earrings.

1. Cut a comfortable length of thread, secure it in the component, and exit a side 4 mm crystal. Pick up three 3 mm bicones, alternating colors A and B, and pass the needle back through the side crystal. Reinforce **[figure 1]**.

2. Work the needle through the design to reach a bicone segment. Pick up three 3 mm bicones, alternating colors A and B, and pass the needle back through the anchor bicone. Reinforce **[figure 2]**.

NOTE: The anchor bicone is the initial bead the needle was exiting before you added new beads.

3. Work the needle down to the component's bottom bicone. Pick up three 3 mm bicones and pass the needle back through the anchor bicone. Reinforce **[figure 3]**.

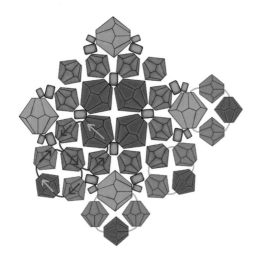

figure 4

4. Work the needle through the design to the next segment of bicones. With the needle exiting the anchor bicone, pick up three 3 mm bicones. Pass the needle back through the anchor bicone. Reinforce **[figure 4].**

5. Work the needle to the next segment of bicones. With the needle exiting the anchor bicone, pick up three 3 mm bicones. Pass the needle through the other end of the anchor bicone. Reinforce **[figure 5]**.

6. To add drops, work the needle to a bicone on the bottom left side of the component. Pick up a 15º seed bead, a cubic zirconia drop, and three 15ºs. Work the needle to a bottom center bicone, pick up three 15ºs, a drop, and three 15ºs. Work the needle to a bottom right bicone, and pick up three 15ºs, a drop, and a 15º **[figure 6]**. Reinforce.

7. For the large loop at the top, work the needle through the design so it is exiting one of the top bicones **[figure 7]**. Pick up: a 15º, an 11º seed bead, a 2 mm round crystal, three 11ºs, a 2 mm round, two 11ºs, a 2 mm round, an 11º, a 15º, an 11º, a 2 mm round, two 11ºs, a 2 mm round, three 11ºs, a 2 mm round, an 11º, and a 15º.

8. Pass the needle through the 3 mm bicone opposite the starting bicone. Reinforce. Weave in excess thread and trim. Open an earwire and attach.

9. Repeat to make a second earring.

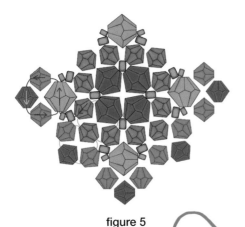

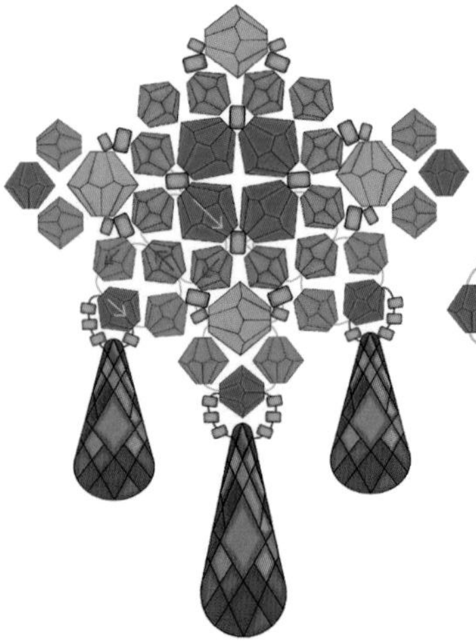

figure 5

figure 6

figure 7

Chandelier Necklace

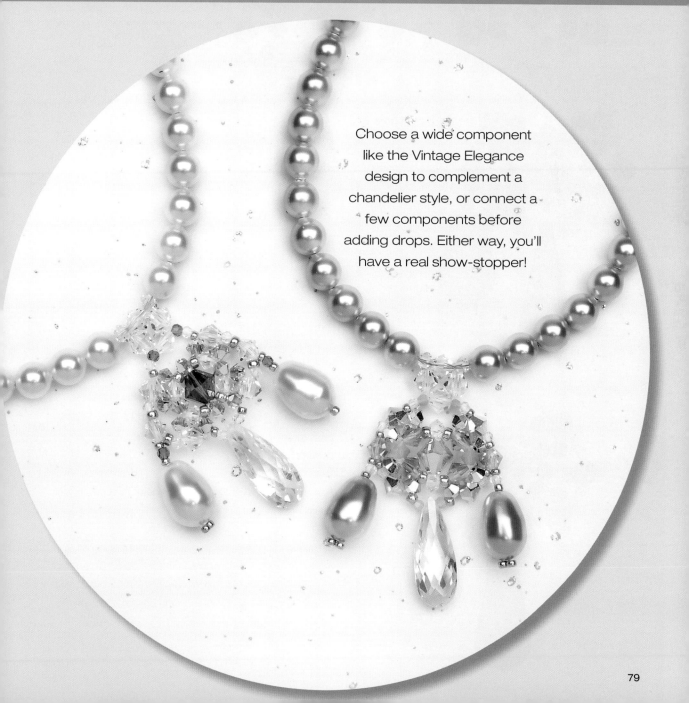

Choose a wide component like the Vintage Elegance design to complement a chandelier style, or connect a few components before adding drops. Either way, you'll have a real show-stopper!

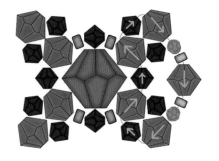

figure 1

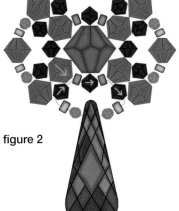

figure 2

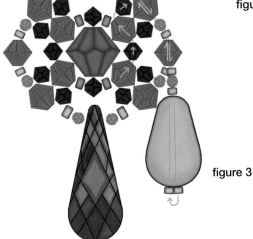

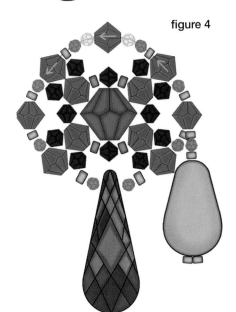

figure 3

figure 4

Supplies

1 component
5 4 mm bicones
2 8 x 11 pearl drops
7 x 18 mm faceted cubic
    zirconia pear drop briolette
12 2 mm round crystals
16-in. (41 cm) strand
    6 mm pearls
15º seed beads
beading wire, .016
clasp
needle, size 12
thread burner

NOTE: I've used the Vintage Elegance component, which needs to be built up before adding the drops; if you choose a different component, you can skip to step 4.

1. Using the working thread or 6–8 in. (15–20 cm) tail (whichever is the longest), exit a side bicone.

2. Pick up one 2 mm round crystal, one 11º seed bead, one 4 mm bicone, one 11º, and one 2 mm round. Pass the needle through the opposite side bicone on the component **[figure 1]**. Reinforce.

3. Weave the needle to the other side of the component and repeat the step 2.

4. Weave the needle through the component to exit a corner bicone on the component. Pick up a 15º, a 2 mm round crystal, a cubic zirconia drop, a 2 mm round, and a 15º. Pass the needle through the 3 mm bicone on the other side **[figure 2]**. Reinforce.

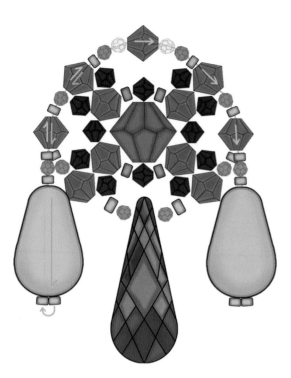

figure 5

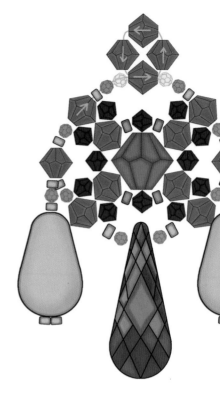

figure 6

5. Weave the needle through the component to exit the side 4 mm bicone added in step 2. Pick up a 15º, a 2 mm round crystal, a 15º, a pearl drop, and two 15ºs. Pass the needle back up through the drop, 11º, 2 mm round, 11º, and 4 mm bicone **[figure 3]**. Reinforce.

6. Weave the needle through the component to exit a top 4 mm bicone. Pick up a 15º, two 2 mm round crystals (same or different colors), a 4 mm bicone, two 2 mm rounds, and one 15º. Pass the needle through the 4 mm bicone **[figure 4]**. Reinforce.

7. Work the needle through the design until it is exiting the 4 mm bicone on the other side. Repeat step 5, then pass the needle halfway through the arch made in step 6 to exit the top 4 mm bicone **[figure 5]**.

8. Pick up three 4 mm bicones and pass the needle back through the bicone in the arch **[figure 6]**. Reinforce.

9. End all the working threads and tails.

10. Turn to "Simply Pearls," p. 58, to string the necklace and complete the pendant.

You don't have to be a movie star to demand attention-grabbing jewels. Stitch large and small Rosette components for eye-catching glamour.

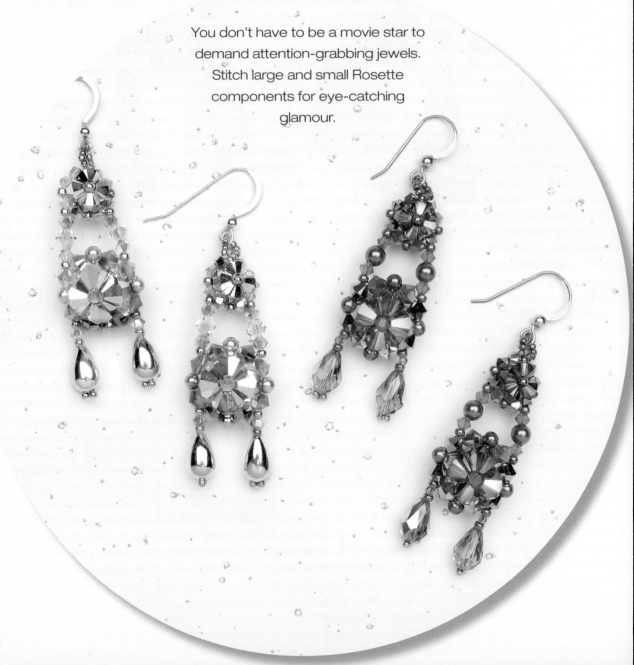

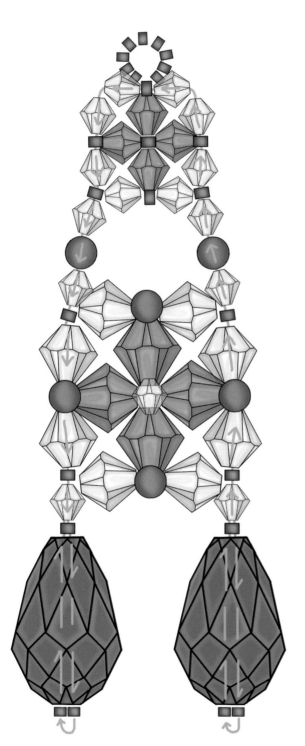

Supplies

4 components, **2** large and
   2 small
4 9 x 6 mm cubic
   zirconia drops
8 3 mm bicones
2 3 mm pearls
15º seed beads
pair of earring findings
needle, size 12
thread burner
2 pairs of chainnose pliers

1. Cut a comfortable length of thread, secure it in the component, and exit one of the bottom sides of a small component. Pick up a 15º seed bead, a 3 mm bicone, a 3 mm pearl, a 3 mm bicone, and a 15º **[figure]**.

2. Pass the needle down through the side of the large design. Pick up a 15º, a 3 mm bicone, a 15º, a CZ drop, and two 15ºs. Go back up through the CZ drop, 15º, 3 mm bicone, and 15º.

3. Pass the needle back up through the components and over to the other side. Repeat steps 1 and 2 on the other side **[figure]**. To reinforce, pass the needle back up and over the design again.

4. Work the needle back to the top of the component. With the needle exiting the top 15º, pick up nine 15º and go back through the 15º in the opposite direction. Reinforce. End the threads.

5. Attach an earring finding and end the threads.

6. Make a second earring.

Sparkling Chandeliers

Make these head-turning accessories to transport yourself back in time. Both the Tudor Romance and Victorian styles evoke images of bygone society and charm.

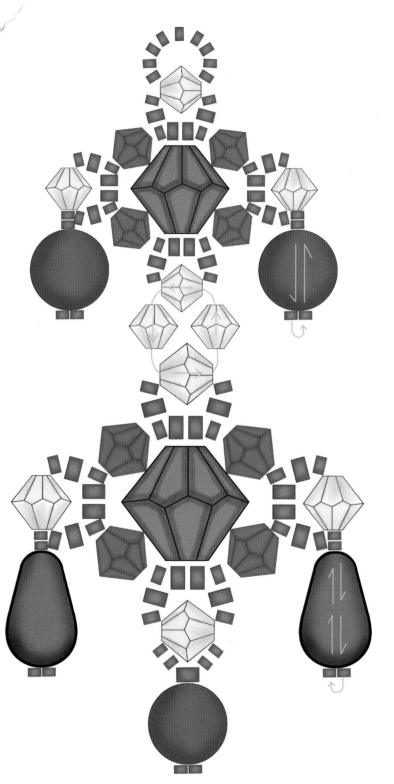

Supplies
4 components, **2** large and
  2 small
6 6 mm pearls
4 4 mm bicones
4 9 x 6 mm sterling silver drops
11º seed beads
15º seed beads
pair of earring findings
FireLine, 4-lb. test
needles, size 12
thread burner
2 pairs of chainnose pliers

1. Using the working thread or 6–8 in. (15–20 cm) tail (whichever is longest), exit a side bicone in a small component. Add a 6 mm pearl following steps 1 and 2 of the "Pearl Drop Earrings," p. 60.

2. Repeat step 1 on the other side of the component.

3. Weave the needle through the component to exit the bottom bicone. Pick up one 4 mm bicone, go through the top bicone in a large component, pick up one 4 mm bicone, and sew back through the bottom bicone in the small component from the opposite direction. Reinforce and end the thread.

4. Using the threads on the large component, add the right silver drop dangle as in step 1.

5. Add the left silver drop dangle as in step 1.

6. Add the bottom pearl dangle the same way. End the threads.

7. Attach the earring finding.

8. Make a second earring to match the first.

Shimmering Headband

If you truly want to shine and stand out from the crowd, this elegant headband is for you. I love the look of soft ribbon against crystals, and I bet you will, too! Use any symmetrical component to complete this piece.

Supplies
9 components
72 6 mm pearls
36 3 mm bicone crystals
48 3 mm pearls
2 2-to-1 connectors
2 9 mm jump rings
4 crimp beads
4 crimp covers
30–35 in. (76–89 cm)
  ¼ in. (6 mm) satin ribbon
flexible beading wire, .019
needle, size 12
scissors
thread burner
2 pairs of chainnose pliers
crimping pliers
wire cutters

1. Decide how many components you would like to connect (I used nine). For a subtle version, use only a few. For a glamorous look, use as many as 10.

2. End the thread in the components. Decide how long the beaded portion of the piece will be, and cut two pieces of beading wire a few inches longer than that length.

3. On one wire, string a pattern of crystals and pearls, then string the top bicone in a component. On the other wire, string the same number of crystals and pearls, along with the bottom bicone of the component.

4. Repeat the previous step with the remaining components. Be sure to string the same number of pearls and crystals between components.

5. To finish, on one strand, string a crimp bead and a loop of the 2-to-1 connector, and go back through the crimp bead. Crimp the crimp bead and cover with a crimp cover. Repeat with the remaining strands and the remaining loops on the 2-to-1 connectors.

6. Attach a jump ring to the remaining end of each 2-to-1 connector, and use an overhand knot to tie a length of ribbon to each jump ring.

Peyote Pendant

Stitch a little something extra with a peyote-strap bail. You can connect the pendant to just about anything: ribbon, cord, chain, or even beaded straps.

figure 1

figure 2

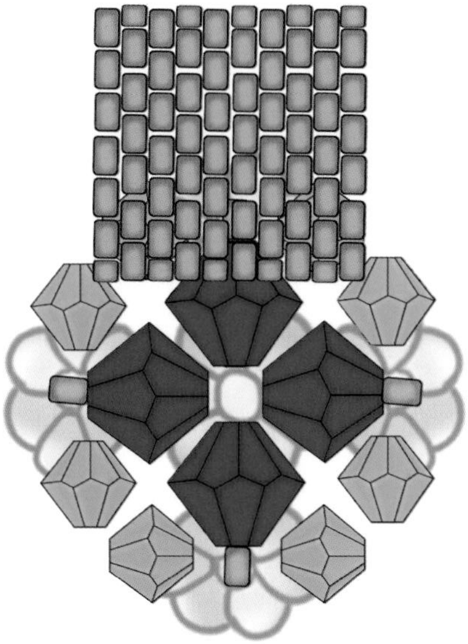

Supplies
1 component
11º cylinder beads
clasp
18–24 in. (48–61 cm)
  stringing material, such
  as ribbon, cord, or chain
FireLine, 4-lb. test
needle, size 12
scissors
thread burner

Try something different

Instead of ribbon, make a thin peyote strap to display the pendant.

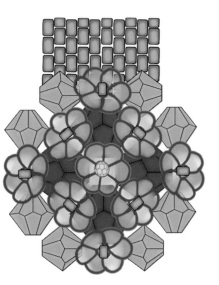

figure 3

figure 4

1. End the working thread and tail on the component. Cut a comfortable length of thread and thread a needle.

2. Weave into the component and exit a top 6 mm bicone. Pick up 10 11º cylinder beads, and pass the needle through the opposite 6 mm bicone **[figure 1]**. Reinforce.

3. Working in peyote stitch, stitch several rows until your strip is large enough to fit the stringing material **[figures 2 and 3]**. Then zip up the first and last rows. End the thread **[figure 4]**.

Elegant Choker

String two strands of glittering style.
The Tudor Romance component
works especially well, but you can
choose any style or color you like!

Supplies

3 components
2 mm round crystals
8 x 11 mm pearl drop
4 9 x 6 mm cubic
   zirconia drops
4 mm bicone crystal
8 3 mm bicone crystals
2 16-in. (41 cm) strands
   4 mm pearls
11º seed beads
2-strand clasp
4 crimp beads
4 crimp covers
flexible beading wire .019
needle, size 12
thread burner
crimping pliers
chainnose pliers
wire cutters

1. End the threads in all of the components. For one component, follow the first two steps of the "Pearl Drop Earrings," p. 60, using 2 mm round crystals instead of seed beads.

2. Decide how long you want your choker to be, and cut two pieces of beading wire to a few inches longer than that length.

3. On one wire, string a pattern of pearls for 5–6 in. (13–15 cm), then string the top bicone of a component.

4. String three pearls, a 3 mm bicone, a 11º seed bead, a cubic zirconia drop, an 11º, a 3 mm bicone, three pearls, and the embellished component from step 1. Repeat to string the final component, then string the same number of pearls and 11ºs as in step 3.

5. Repeat steps 3 and 4 on the other wire, stringing the lower bicones in the component. The lower strand will need to have a few more beads so the choker drapes properly. Check the fit periodically as you string the beads and components to make sure it will hang nicely on your neck.

6. On each end of one strand, string a crimp bead and a loop of half of the clasp. Go back through the crimp bead and a few pearls, crimp the crimp bead, and cover with a crimp cover. Trim the excess wire. Repeat with the remaining strand and the remaining loops on the clasp.

Centerpiece Ring

If you have a gorgeous crystal design, a simple ring band is the perfect way to show it off. Display any of the components in this book in style!

Supplies

1 component
26–32 3 mm round beads
mix of 11º seed beads, 15º
   seed beads, 2 mm round
   crystals, or 3 mm bicones
FireLine, 4-lb. test
needle, size 12
scissors
thread burner

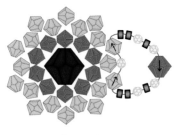

figure 1

figure 2

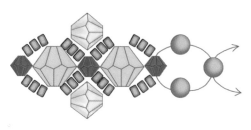

figure 3

figure 4

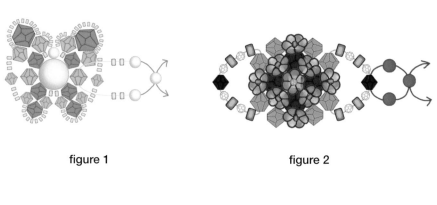

figure 5

figure 6

figure 7

NOTE: Figures 1–12 show the best thread paths to follow for each component in the book.

1. End the working thread and tail in the component.

2. Cut about 30 in. (76 cm) of thread and thread both ends with a needle.

3. Pass one of the needles through a side crystal (or two or three, depending on the shape of the component). Center the component on the thread.

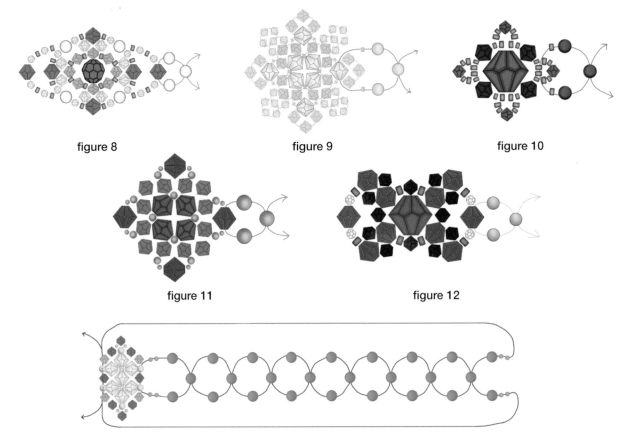

figure 8

figure 9

figure 10

figure 11

figure 12

figure 13

4. With each needle, pick up a few crystals and seed beads as desired [**figures 1–12**].

5. With one needle, pick up one 3 mm round bead. Pass the other needle through the bead, going in the opposite direction. Repeat until the beadwork can wrap comfortably around your finger [**figure 13**].

6. For the last stitch, with each needle pick up the same types of beads used in step 4. Pass both needles through the crystal(s) on the other side of the component, passing the needles in opposite directions.

7. Reinforce the band by weaving the thread back and forth through it, one needle at a time. End the threads.

Try something different

Embellish your ring band with 4–8 2 mm round crystals instead of round beads, if you like.

From the author

This might not be a "normal" thank you page, but all of these souls matter to me!

This book is dedicated in loving memory of my father, Floyd Thomas Carpenter, Jr., who is now enjoying his extended golf vacation, no doubt; my "adopted dad" Bob Oehlbeck; Grandma Heimbach; Clowey; and precious and loving Tigger (Tig Pig).

A special thank you to my family and friends: My mother, Joanne Carpenter, sister, Tammy Parker, and aunt Gloria Dragon have all supported me through so much. Thanks to my adopted family, Brian Broxton, Suzzanne Oehlbeck, Bonnie Heimbach and Leigh Ann Mobarik, Fran Beasley, and Patsy and Wayne Hall, as well.

Without the encouragement of White Fox Beads Studio owner Gail DeLuca and employees Michelle Gibson, Jessica Carmichael, Kathy Horne, and Pam Guthrie, this book might never have come to be. Thanks also to Janice "The Mineral Lady," Pat Hollenbeck, Barbara Romano, Greta Smith, and Dr. Joseph Payne.

Thanks to Kalmbach and my editor, Erica Swanson, for believing in me and giving me this opportunity.

Lastly, thanks to my cats, Buffy, Nubbie, Princess Buttercup, and Mr. Winky; Jack the beagle; and my extended furry family (Reilly and Charlie). All of our pets were strays, and I am glad that they chose to adopt us.

About the Author

Aimee Carpenter has lived all over the U.S. and currently calls Tennessee home. She graduated from the Savannah College of Art and Design in 1999 with a B.F.A. in Graphic Design and learned all of her beading skills at the White Fox Bead Studio in Maryville, Tenn., her favorite shop. It wasn't long before Aimee started creating her own designs. Her favorite medium is Swarovski crystals. Aimee teaches classes and is known to her friends and customers at the shop as Lil' Miss Sparkley. She has an Etsy shop of the same name where you can see some of her work.

To contact Aimee, visit her Etsy shop at: www.etsy.com/shop/LilMissSparkley and send her a message.

Resources

White Fox Bead Studio,
Maryville, Tenn.
www.white-fox-bead-studio.com

Fusion Beads
www.FusionBeads.com

Flowerchylde's Bead & Things
ebay store: Flowerchyldes-Beads
Etsy: www.Flowerchylde.etsy.com

Beadaholique
www.beadaholique.com

The Ribbon Retreat
www.RibbonRetreat.com

Customize Your Jewelry with These Innovative Ideas!

Crystal Brilliance

The romance of crystals is captured in this magnificent collection from *Bead&Button* associate editor Anna Elizabeth Draeger. Showcasing the brilliance and breathtaking hues of CRYSTALLIZED™ – Swarovski Elements in 26 projects, this book also offers creative variations like alternate colors and coordinating earrings. The fantastic designs, combined with the reliable instructions readers love, make this a must-have resource.
62953 $21.95

Making Elegant Jewelry for Special Occasions
Special occasions deserve significant jewelry! Here you'll find 30 projects for celebrating life's landmark events with stylish, sophisticated pieces that add the perfect finishing touch with sparkling crystals, delicate wire, and luminous pearls. 64254 $17.95

Cube Bead Stitching
Seed bead style in squares! This book includes a variety of projects, from small pieces that work up quickly to stunning necklaces, appealing to beaders of all skill levels. Chapters are divided by project type: bracelets, earrings, necklaces, rings, and decorative items. 62816 $19.95

Your Seed Bead Style
Variety is the name of the game in this fun, inspiring book! Over 30 projects show you how to incorporate interesting materials into basic seed bead jewelry. Organized by material, it features a variety of techniques and stitches including peyote, herringbone, square stitch, bead embroidery, tatting, right-angle weave, and more. 62847 $17.95